CLASSIC *f*M

Friendly

Music Quiz Book

CLASSIC *f*M

Friendly

Music Quiz Book

Darren Henley

Hodder Arnold

www.hoddereducation.com

For UK order enquiries: please contact Bookpoint Ltd, 130 Milton Park, Abingdon, Oxon OX14 4SB. Telephone: +44(0) 1235 827720. Fax: +44(0) 1235 400454. Lines are open 09.00–17.00, Monday to Saturday, with a 24-hour message answering service. You can also order through our website www.hoddereducation.com

British Library Cataloguing in Publication Data: a catalogue record for this title is available from the British Library.

First published in UK 2007, by Hodder Education, a member of the Hodder Headline Group, an Hachette Livre UK Company, 338 Euston Road, London NW1 3BH.

Copyright © 2007 Darren Henley

Typeset by Servis Filmsetting Ltd, Manchester
Printed in Great Britain by Cox & Wyman Ltd, Reading, Berkshire.

Hodder Headline's policy is to use papers that are natural, renewable and recyclable products and made from wood grown in sustainable forests. The logging and manufacturing processes are expected to conform to the environmental regulations of the country of origin.

Impression number   10 9 8 7 6 5 4 3 2

Year   2011 2010 2009 2008

ISBN 978 0340 95715 8

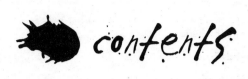

contents

Contents

A Friendly Word Before We Get Started . . .

If you listen hard enough, classical music is everywhere, all around us. We're just as likely to hear it on television, at the cinema, at football grounds and in restaurants as we are on CD, in the concert hall or by listening to a classical music radio station such as Classic FM.

This is the fifth book in our *Classic FM Friendly* Series. We've already published *The Classic FM Friendly Guide to Music*, which takes the reader from classical music's earliest incarnations right

through to the present day. Alongside that, there are more in-depth guides to the lives and music of Wolfgang Amadeus Mozart, Ludwig van Beethoven and Sir Edward Elgar. The *Friendly* book that you are reading now exists in its own right as a quiz book, but can also act as a companion volume to the others in the series.

We've set out to create the classical music quiz book that has something for everyone. So, no matter if you are still just dipping a toe gingerly into the classical music waters, or if you have been basking in all of classical music's glories for years; you will find questions that you can answer in the next one hundred or so pages.

How does the *Classic FM Friendly Music Quiz Book* work?

The book is made up of 1,000 questions, divided into a series of rounds. As you will see, some of the rounds require straight general knowledge about classical music; other rounds use a number of tried and tested quiz formats, such as working on the basis of mixing and matching answers given on the page, or by asking whether statements are true or false. We have graded all of the Quick Fire rounds as being *Friendly*, *Enthusiastic* or *Fiendish*, depending on the level of difficulty we believe you will have in answering the question. You will find that the *Friendly* rounds of this type are towards the front of the book, with the *Fiendish* ones being towards the back.

Once you've answered all of the questions, you can score yourself by checking out the answers section at the back of the book.

Good luck! And remember the old adage that any quiz question is easy . . . as long as you know the answer.

The Questions

Quick Fire (*Friendly*)

1 If "legato" is a request by a composer to a performer to play their music smoothly, what does "staccato" mean?
2 What does the word "opera" actually mean?
3 Tchaikovsky's *1812 Overture* celebrates the victory of which nation over which other nation?
4 What is the name of the piece of instrumental music played at the beginning of an opera, which often includes musical themes heard later on?
5 What are the names of The Three Tenors?
6 Which flautist became known as "the man with the golden flute" in the 1970s and 1980s?
7 "Piano" is short for the Italian word "pianoforte". What does that translate as?
8 In the popular children's story by Paul Tripp, what sort of instrument is Tubby?
9 Leonard Bernstein wrote the music to *West Side Story*. Who wrote the words?
10 In which Suffolk seaside town, where he founded a music festival, did Benjamin Britten make his home?

11 Who is the current Master of the Queen's Music?

12 In 2007, his 150th birthday year, the Bank of England decided to take Sir Edward Elgar off the back of the 20-pound note. With whom did they replace him?

13 Spell the Polish composer Henryk Górecki's surname phonetically.

14 How many symphonies did Joseph Haydn compose?

15 He's famous now as a classical composer, but of which 1970s rock band was Karl Jenkins a member?

16 What family relationship did Felix and Fanny Mendelssohn have?

17 Which was written first – Frédéric Chopin's Piano Concerto No. 1 or his Piano Concerto No. 2?

18 Name the piece of music composed by Maurice Ravel, which was made famous when Torvill and Dean won a gold medal at the 1984 Olympic Games in Sarajevo.

19 The dish Tournedos Rossini was named after the composer Gioachino Rossini. It consists of croutons with steak layered on top, along with which two other toppings?

20 In which English city is the composer John Rutter based?

02

Cinematic Sounds

Match the film soundtrack composers to their films:

You can choose from:

49th Parallel; Alien; Dances with Wolves; Dangerous Moonlight; The Gadfly; Gladiator; The Heiress; Henry V; The Hours; Lieutenant Kijé; The Lord of the Rings; The Magnificent Seven; The Mission; The Piano; Pride and Prejudice; Robin Hood, Prince of Thieves; Sense and Sensibility; The Snowman; Superman; Titanic.

1 Richard Addinsell
2 John Barry
3 Elmer Bernstein
4 Howard Blake
5 Aaron Copland
6 Carl Davis
7 Patrick Doyle
8 Philip Glass
9 Jerry Goldsmith
10 James Horner

Quick Fire (*Friendly*)

1 Which of Schubert's symphonies is known as being *Unfinished*?

2 What musical jobs did Robert Schumann's wife, Clara, do?

3 Who was known as "the Father of the Waltz"?

4 Who was known as "the Waltz King"?

5 Classic FM's first Composer in Residence, Joby Talbot, was once a member of which pop group?

6 By what nickname was Antonio Vivaldi known?

7 John Tavener and John Taverner are both English composers, but one was born around 450 years earlier than the other. Which was it?

8 Gregorian Chant was named after whom?

9 What is the name of the 12th-century nun who, as well as being a composer, also wrote poetry and was a famed mystic, having no fewer than 26 visions?

10 We talk about Renaissance music, but what is the literal translation of "Renaissance" from French into English?

11 The Belgian Early Music composer Guillaume Dufay wrote a mass based on a folk song called *The Armed Man*. What is the name of the 21st-century Welsh composer who had great success with his new work of the same name?

12 The early English composer John Taverner was friendly
with the man who was one of the main forces behind
the dissolution of the monasteries. What was the name
of his friend?

13 What does "opus" literally mean?

14 Which body decreed that anybody who made an illegal
copy of Gregorio Allegri's *Miserere* would be punished?

15 How did the composer Jean-Baptiste Lully die?

16 A piece written by the French composer Marc-Antoine
Charpentier is always played at the beginning of the
Eurovision Song Contest. What is its name?

17 The composer Arcangelo Corelli was the master of a
particular type of concerto, where the orchestra is
divided into two groups. One group of musicians tends
to play first, with a second group then echoing the
music played by the first set. What is this sort of
concerto called?

18 "*Frère Jacques*", "*Three Blind Mice*" and "*London's
Burning*" all have something in common with Johann
Pachelbel's most famous work. What is it?

19 What is the first line of *Dido's Lament* from Henry
Purcell's opera *Dido and Aeneas*?

20 On which record label did Nigel Kennedy release his
world famous version of Vivaldi's *Four Seasons*?

The Year in Question

Each of these pairs of events – one musical and one non-musical – took place in the same year in the 1700s. But what was the year in question? To help you, the answers are in chronological order – and the same year appears twice!

1 Antonio Vivaldi is ordained a priest in Venice. – Peter the Great founds St Petersburg.

2 George Frideric Handel's opera *Rinaldo* is performed at the Queen's Theatre in London. – The *Spectator* is founded in London.

3 George Frideric Handel's *Water Music* is performed on a barge on the River Thames. – England's first freemasonic Grand Lodge is founded in London.

4 The original Royal Academy of Music opens in London. – The "South Sea Bubble" bursts, leaving many investors penniless.

5 Johann Sebastian Bach's *St John Passion* is given its first performance in Leipzig. – Immanuel Kant is born.

6 George Frideric Handel becomes a naturalized British subject. – Sir Isaac Newton dies.

7 Johann Sebastian Bach's *St Matthew Passion* is given its first performance in its entirety in Leipzig. – The last execution for witchcraft takes place in Scotland.

8 Giovanni Battista Pergolesi finishes his best-known work, the *Stabat Mater*. – First recorded use of a bathing machine in an engraving by John Setterington.

9 Antonio Vivaldi gets into trouble with the Catholic church because of his failure to say mass, and his close relationship with a young soprano. – The War of Jenkins' Ear begins between England and Spain.

10 Joseph Haydn becomes a choirboy at the court chapel in Vienna. – Frederick the Great's reign begins in Prussia.

11 George Frideric Handel's *Messiah* receives its premiere. – Anders Celsius invents the centigrade thermometer.

12 George Frideric Handel has an operation on his eyes at Guy's Hospital in London. It is not a success. – Britain adopts the Gregorian calendar.

13 Wolfgang Amadeus Mozart is born in Salzburg. – More than 100 British soldiers die in the "Black Hole of Calcutta".

14 Aged 74, George Frideric Handel dies in London. – James Brindley designs the Worsley–Manchester Canal.

15 Wolfgang Amadeus Mozart gives his first concert in Italy, in the city of Verona. – James Hargreaves patents the spinning jenny.

16 Wolfgang Amadeus Mozart marries Constanze Weber in Vienna. – The hot air balloon is invented by the Montgolfier brothers.

17 Wolfgang Amadeus Mozart's opera *The Marriage of Figaro* receives its premiere in Vienna. – Robert Burns's *Poems Chiefly in the Scottish Dialect* is published.

18 Niccolò Paganini makes his debut in Genoa. He is just 11 years old. – Slavery is abolished in the French colonies.

9

19 Franz Schubert and Gaetano Donizetti are born. –
Samuel Taylor Coleridge's *Kubla Khan* is published.

20 Joseph Haydn's *The Creation* is given its premiere in
Vienna. – Napoleon becomes First Consul.

Order! Order!

Johann Sebastian Bach had 20 children. Can you put them in the correct chronological birth order?

1 Carl Philipp Emanuel
2 Catherina Dorothea
3 Christian Gottlieb
4 Christiana Benedicta
5 Christiana Dorothea
6 Christiane Sophie Henriette
7 Elisabeth Juliane Friederike
8 Ernst Andreas
9 Gottfried Heinrich
10 Johann August Abraham
11 Johann Christian
12 Johann Christoph
13 Johann Christoph Friedrich
14 Johann Gottfried Bernhard
15 Johanna Carolina
16 Leopold August
17 Maria Sophia
18 Regine Johanna
19 Regine Susanna
20 Wilhelm Friedemann

Quick Fire *(Friendly)*

1 Johann Sebastian Bach wrote two *Passions* named after which saints?

2 Johann Sebastian Bach believed that 14 was his own personal number. How did he arrive at this figure?

3 George Frideric Handel's father wasn't keen on him learning an instrument, so where did the boy's mother hide his harpsichord so that he could practise out of earshot?

4 George Frideric Handel's boss, the Elector of Hanover, eventually became the English monarch. What was his title?

5 Where is the body of George Frideric Handel buried?

6 Which Austrian town was the 18th-century composer Karl Ditters von Dittersdorf from?

7 For which nobleman did Wolfgang Amadeus Mozart's father work?

8 The film *Amadeus* suggests that Wolfgang Amadeus Mozart was murdered by which composer?

9 Just outside which city was Wolfgang Amadeus Mozart buried in an unmarked grave?

10 Which soprano is known as the "Doncaster Diva"?

11 Who was the first English composer to top the Classic
   FM Hall of Fame?

12 Where did Ludwig van Beethoven's ancestors originally
   come from?

13 What is the name of Ludwig van Beethoven's only
   opera?

14 Radio was born when Marconi successfully sent a
   message by wireless to a receiver over a mile away.
   During which period of classical music did this happen?

15 Nikolai Rimsky-Korsakov's family always expected him
   to go into a particular branch of the armed forces. Was
   it the army, navy or air force?

16 Upon which story is Nikolai Rimsky-Korsakov's greatest
   work, *Scheherezade*, based?

17 What nationality was the composer Bedřich Smetana?

18 Over what item of furnishing in the Savoy Theatre did
   W.S. Gilbert and Arthur Sullivan dramatically fall out?

19 Which city, home of Classic FM's orchestra in the
   North-West, is European Capital of Culture in 2008?

20 In which English county was Sir Edward Elgar born?

True or False?

Decide whether each of these statements is True or False. But be warned, in an attempt to catch you out, some of the details have only been changed very slightly.

1 Ludwig van Beethoven liked to claim that the "van" in the middle of his name meant that he came from noble stock, but in fact he was descended from a perfectly ordinary family.

2 Niccolò Paganini would sometimes snap some of the strings of his violin mid-performance – and was still able to play brilliantly.

3 When he was a boy, Niccolò Paganini's father would punish him for not practising his music, by withdrawing food and water.

4 The composer Charles-Henri Alkan died after a shelf full of books fell on top of him.

5 The composer Ernest Chausson died after a cycling accident.

6 The composer Anton von Webern died after being shot dead for unwittingly breaking an evening curfew at the end of the Second World War.

7 Some harps have pedals.

8 A piccolo is a large version of a flute.

9 A sackbut is an early version of a cello.

10 The last castrato, Alessandro Moreschi, was still singing at the Sistine Chapel in the Vatican until his retirement in 1973.

11 The real name of the soprano Maria Callas was Maria Kalogeropoulos.

12 The conductor Daniel Barenboim is also famous as a renowned cellist.

13 Felix Mendelssohn may have been famous for his *Scottish Symphony* and his *Hebrides Overture*, but he never actually set foot on Scottish soil.

14 Frédéric Chopin is best known for his compositions for the violin.

15 The woman who is regarded as the love of Frédéric Chopin's life often used to strut about the streets of Paris, wearing men's clothes and smoking a large cigar.

16 Franz Liszt was very skilled at turning other people's big tunes into works for the piano. These included pieces by Beethoven, Berlioz, Rossini and Schubert.

17 Despite taking holy orders, Franz Liszt continued to enjoy a string of sexual conquests.

18 Mikhail Glinka's first job was as a civil servant in the Russian Ministry of Communications.

19 Alexander Borodin was the illegitimate son of a Georgian prince.

20 Despite coming from a wealthy background and having huge talent, both as a composer and as a pianist, Sergei Rachmaninov died in drink-induced poverty at the age of just 42.

Quick Fire (*Friendly*)

1 How is Sir Edward Elgar's *Variations on a Theme* now better known?

2 Translate *"Nessun Dorma"* into English.

3 Which rock superstar had a hit in 2006 with an album of works by the 16th-century composer, singer and lutenist John Dowland?

4 Claude Debussy completed *La Mer* while staying at which English seaside resort?

5 Give a word which rhymes with the correct pronunciation of Ralph Vaughan Williams's first name.

6 What is the name of the only piano work ever to top the Classic FM Hall of Fame?

7 At which London school was Gustav Holst the Director of Music for many years, even writing a suite dedicated to the place?

8 In which English city was Frederick Delius born?

9 What unusual event occurred at the premiere of Igor Stravinsky's ballet *The Rite of Spring*?

10 Sergei Prokofiev died on the same day as a Russian leader who had done an enormous amount to suppress his music. Who was that leader?

11 Francis Poulenc's father was a wealthy chemist who owned a pharmaceutical company. What was its name?

12 Which George Gershwin opera includes the hits *"Summertime"* and *"I got plenty o' Nuttin'"*?

13 When William Walton was 19, he wrote *Façade* as an accompaniment to whose rather outlandish and highly theatrical poetry?

14 One of Dmitri Shostakovich's songs was sung over the radio back to mission control by which Russian cosmonaut?

15 What is the name of the work by John Cage that consists of around four-and-a-half minutes of silence?

16 John Tavener owes the release of his *Celtic Requiem* on Apple Records to which member of The Beatles?

17 In which building was the premiere performance of *Paul McCartney's Liverpool Oratorio* given?

18 What was the name of the choral work in four movements by Sir Paul McCartney that received its premiere in the Royal Albert Hall in London at the end of 2006?

19 What was the name of the debut UK album by the New Zealand star Hayley Westenra?

20 What job did the tenor Alfie Boe do before he changed careers and became an opera singer?

09

Birthday Bonanza

Match the year of their birth to each composer:

> ### You can choose from:
>
> *John Barry; Béla Bartók; Georges Bizet; Alexander Borodin; Carl Philipp Emanuel Bach; Johann Christian Bach; Karl Ditters von Dittersdorf; Marc-Antoine Charpentier; Mikhail Glinka; George Frideric Handel; Karl Jenkins; Sergei Rachmaninov; Joaquín Rodrigo; Gioachino Rossini; Camille Saint-Saëns; Howard Shore; Johann Strauss Jr; Joby Talbot; Georg Philipp Telemann; Richard Wagner.*

1 1643
2 1681
3 1685
4 1714
5 1735
6 1739
7 1792
8 1804
9 1813
10 1825

11 1833
12 1835
13 1838
14 1873
15 1881
16 1901
17 1933
18 1944
19 1946
20 1971

They Said What?

The greatest classical composers have never been backward in coming forward. Do you know which hallowed composers made each of these often not so hallowed utterances?

1 "It's easy to play any musical instrument: all you have to do is touch the right key at the right time and the instrument will play itself."

2 "One should try everything once, except incest and folk-dancing."

3 "Rossini would have been a great composer if his teacher had spanked him enough on the backside."

4 "If she can strike a low G or F like a death-rattle and high F like the shriek of a little dog when you step on its tail, the house will resound with acclamations."

5 "I am not interested in having an orchestra sound like itself. I want it to sound like the composer."

6 "If there is anyone here whom I have not insulted, I beg his pardon."

7 "That old idea . . . of a composer suddenly having a terrific idea and sitting up all night to write it is nonsense. Night time is for sleeping."

8 "Listening to the fifth symphony of Ralph Vaughan Williams is like staring at a cow for 45 minutes."

9 "Never compose anything unless not composing it becomes a positive nuisance to you."

10 "Modern music is as dangerous as cocaine."

11 "I write as a sow piddles."

12 "I'm not handsome, but when women hear me play, they come crawling to my feet."

13 "A good conductor ought to be a good chauffeur. The qualities that make the one also make the other. They are concentration, an incessant control of attention, and presence of mind – the conductor only has to add a little sense of music."

14 "I'm told that Saint-Saëns has informed a delighted public that since the war began he has composed music for the stage, melodies, an elegy and a piece for the trombone. If he'd been making shell-cases instead it might have been all the better for music."

15 "Give me a laundry list and I will set it to music."

16 "In order to compose, all you have to do is think of a tune that nobody else has thought of."

17 "Pay no attention to what the critics say. No statue has ever been put up to a critic."

18 "Never look at the trombones, it only encourages them."

19 "Too many pieces of music finish too long after the end."

20 "Truly there would be reason to go mad if it were not for music."

Mix & Match

Joseph Haydn wrote a total of 104 symphonies. Many of them acquired nicknames. Can you match the number of each symphony with its nickname?

You can choose from:

The Bear; Clock; The Distracted; Drum Roll; Farewell; Fire; The Hen; The Hunt; Lamentation; London; Maria Theresa; Mercury; Military; Miracle; Oxford; The Passion; The Philosopher; The Queen; The Schoolmaster; Surprise.

1 No. 22 in E flat
2 No. 26 in D minor
3 No. 43 in E flat
4 No. 45 in F sharp minor
5 No. 48 in C
6 No. 49 in F minor
7 No. 55 in E flat
8 No. 59 in A
9 No. 60 in C
10 No. 73 in D

11 No. 82 in C
12 No. 83 in G minor
13 No. 85 in B flat
14 No. 92 in G
15 No. 94 in G
16 No. 96 in D
17 No. 100 in G
18 No. 101 in D
19 No. 103 in E flat
20 No. 104 in D

Order! Order!

Put these musical speeds into the correct order, slowest to fastest:

1 Adagio
2 Andante
3 Allegretto
4 Allegro
5 Largo
6 Presto

Put these voices in the correct order, highest to lowest:

1 Baritone
2 Bass
3 Bass-baritone
4 Mezzo-soprano
5 Soprano
6 Tenor

Put these Masters of the King's or Queen's Music into the correct order, first to last:

1 Arnold Bax
2 Arthur Bliss
3 William Boyce
4 Edward Elgar
5 Nicholas Lanier
6 Peter Maxwell Davies

Put Mozart's Christian names in the correct order:

1 Amadeus
2 Chrysostomus
3 Johannes
4 Wolfgangus

Mix & Match

Match the concert hall to the town or city:

> ## You can choose from:
>
> *Aldeburgh; Amsterdam; Basingstoke; Belfast; Birmingham; Cardiff; Croydon; Edinburgh; Gateshead; Glasgow; Leipzig; Liverpool; London; Los Angeles; Manchester; New York; Poole; Vienna; Washington; Zürich.*

1 The Barbican
2 The Philharmonic Hall
3 Concertgebauw
4 Carnegie Hall
5 Walt Disney Concert Hall
6 Usher Hall
7 The Sage
8 The Lighthouse
9 St David's Hall
10 The Bridgewater Hall

11 Symphony Hall
12 Musikverein
13 The Anvil
14 The Waterfront
15 Snape Maltings
16 Gewandhaus
17 Tonhalle
18 Fairfield Halls
19 Kennedy Center
20 Royal Concert Hall

The Year in Question

Each of these pairs of events – one musical and one non-musical – took place in the same year in the 1800s. But what was the year in question? To help you, the answers are in chronological order.

1 Ludwig van Beethoven's *Symphony No. 1* is performed in Vienna. – Invention of the first chemical battery by Alessandro Volta.

2 Franz Liszt is born. – Jane Austen's *Sense and Sensibility* is published.

3 The Royal Philharmonic Society is founded in London. – Jane Austen's *Pride and Prejudice* is published.

4 Franz Schubert composes his first song using a text by Goethe. It's called *"Gretchen at the Spinning Wheel"*. – Stephenson designs his first steam locomotive, the *Blücher*.

5 Gioachino Rossini signs a contract to write *The Barber of Seville* in December. It will receive its premiere early in the following year. – Napoleon is defeated at the Battle of Waterloo.

6 Jacques Offenbach is born in Cologne. – The USA buys Florida from Spain.

7 Gioachino Rossini travels to England. He is welcomed by King George IV on a visit to Brighton. – Mexico is made a republic.

8 Richard Wagner writes his first complete opera. It's called *The Fairies*. – Slavery is outlawed in the British Empire.

9 Frédéric Chopin invents a new type of piano tune, the *Ballade*. – The first instalment of Charles Dickens's *Pickwick Papers* is published.

10 Max Bruch is born in Cologne and Georges Bizet is born in Paris. – Grace Darling and her father rescue nine people from the wreck of the *Forfarshire*.

11 Pyotr Ilyich Tchaikovsky is born in Russia and Niccolò Paganini dies in France. – Warren de la Rue passes an electric current through a coil in a vacuum tube and demonstrates the first electric light bulb.

12 The Vienna Philharmonic Orchestra is founded. – China hands over Hong Kong to Great Britain.

13 Felix Mendelssohn finishes his one and only *Violin Concerto*. – The first telegraph message is transmitted.

14 Richard Wagner's opera *Tannhäuser* gets its first performance in Dresden, but not everyone regards it as a big hit. – Dumas's *The Count of Monte Cristo* is published.

15 Robert Schumann's only *Piano Concerto* is given its debut performance in Leipzig. Clara Schumann is the soloist. – The sewing machine is patented.

16 Felix Mendelssohn conducts *Elijah* in London, Manchester and Birmingham, but tragedy strikes when his sister Fanny dies shortly afterwards. – The Brontë sisters are busy: Charlotte's *Jane Eyre* and Emily's *Wuthering Heights* are both published.

17 Hector Berlioz gives a concert in London on 29 June and Frédéric Chopin spends a few months in the city, giving a series of concerts, culminating in a performance on 16 November. – Ireland suffers from the potato famine, but California fares better: gold is discovered at Sutter's Mill and the Gold Rush is on.

18 Frédéric Chopin's own *Funeral March* is played at his funeral in Paris. – Charles Dickens's *David Copperfield* is published.

19 Giuseppe Verdi's opera *Il Trovatore* receives its premiere in Rome and his *La Traviata* gets its first public outing in Venice. – The first railway between New York and Chicago opens.

20 Robert Schumann attempts to commit suicide by throwing himself into the River Rhine. – The Charge of the Light Brigade takes place as part of the Crimean War.

Whose Aria is it Anyway?

From which opera was each of these famous arias or choruses taken?

1 *"Celeste Aida"*
2 *"Largo al Factotum"*
3 *"O soave fanciulla"*
4 *Toreador's Song*
5 *The Flower Duet*
6 *"Voi che sapete"*
7 *Chorus of the Hebrew Slaves*
8 *"Au fond du temple saint"*
9 *"When I am laid in earth"*
10 *"Sempre Libera"*
11 *The Willow Song*
12 *Song to The Moon*
13 *"Casta Diva"*
14 *"Nessun Dorma"*
15 *"La ci darem la mano"*
16 *"O welche Lust"*
17 *"O mio babbino caro"*
18 *Easter Hymn*
19 *"Vissi d'arte"*
20 *"It ain't necessarily so"*

Definitive Mix & Match

Match the musical term to its definition:

> ### You can choose from:
>
> *a capella; adagio; allegro; aria; cadenza; chamber music; concerto; gavotte; intermezzo; legato; libretto; Lieder; Kappelmeister; movement; opus; oratorio; quartet; quintet; toccata; trio.*

1 A piece of music written for three players.
2 A religious work featuring soloists, a choir and orchestra. Sometimes acted out, but usually without scenery or costumes.
3 Unaccompanied choral singing.
4 A piece of music written for five players.
5 The Italian instruction from a composer to a performer to play the music in a lively and bright way.
6 A piece of music written for keyboard, where the performer will often have to play both very quickly and very delicately.
7 A solo song from an opera.
8 Music that was originally designed to be played by small instrumental groups in people's homes rather than in churches or concert halls.

9 An orchestral piece that features a starring role for the player of one particular instrument, who usually sits out at the front of the stage, next to the conductor.

10 An old French dance.

11 The Italian instruction from a composer to a performer to play the music smoothly.

12 The words of an opera.

13 The music director of a nobleman's choir.

14 A piece of music written for four players.

15 An individual section of a bigger work such as a concerto or a symphony.

16 An instrumental interlude in the middle of an opera, used to show that time has passed by between two bits of action on stage.

17 Often used as the name of the slow movement of a classical work.

18 A musical work, often followed by a number for cataloguing purposes.

19 An improvised section, usually towards the end of a work, which gives the soloist a chance to show off.

20 A type of German solo song, often performed with a piano as accompaniment.

Name that Composer

Each of the groups of works below was written by one person. Can you name that composer?

1 *Abdelazer; Trumpet Tune and Air in D; Come Ye Sons of Art*

2 *Four Seasons; Gloria; "Nulla in Mundo Pax Sincera"*

3 *Brandenburg Concertos; Goldberg Variations; Toccata and Fugue in D minor*

4 *Water Music; Solomon; Xerxes*

5 *The Creation; The Seasons; Symphony No. 94 (the "Surprise")*

6 *Laudate Dominum; Requiem; Clarinet Concerto in A*

7 *Fidelio; Für Elise; Moonlight Sonata*

8 *March Militaire No. 1; Piano Quintet ("Trout"); Rosamunde*

9 *Symphonie Fantastique; The Childhood of Christ; Requiem*

10 *O for the Wings of a Dove; Songs without Words; A Midsummer Night's Dream*

11 Nocturne No. 2; Prelude No. 15 ("The Raindrop");
    Waltz No. 6 (The "Minute" Waltz)

12 Scenes from Childhood No. 7 – Dreaming; Fantasie in
    C; Dichterliebe

13 Hungarian Rhapsody No. 2; Liebestraum No. 3;
    Rhapsodie Espagnole

14 The Pearl Fishers; L'Arlésienne Suite No. 1; Jeux
    d'Enfants

15 A Life for the Tsar; Ruslan and Ludmilla; Kamarinskya

16 Prince Igor; In the Steppes of Central Asia; String
    Quartet No. 2

17 Night on the Bare Mountain; Pictures at an Exhibition;
    Boris Godunov

18 Scheherezade; Flight of the Bumble Bee; Capriccio
    Espagnol

19 The Nutcracker; 1812 Overture; Swan Lake

20 Rusalka; Serenade for Strings; Slavonic Dances

Quick Fire (*Enthusiastic*)

1 Which animal does the double bass represent in the *Carnival of the Animals* by Camille Saint-Saëns?

2 Who wrote the music to the children's classic *Babar the Elephant*?

3 Edvard Grieg wrote his *Peer Gynt Suite* as the incidental music to a play of the same name by which Norwegian writer?

4 Which Irish composer is said to have invented the Nocturne?

5 What does Cor Anglais translate as?

6 The late Jack Brymer was the principal clarinettist with which orchestra from 1971 until his retirement?

7 The Prince of Wales has recently re-introduced the tradition of having a harpist as a member of his court. What was the name of the first person he appointed to this position?

8 What was the name of the Belgian who invented the saxophone?

9 Legend has it that Johann Sebastian Bach walked four hundred or so miles to hear which organist play?

10 Which English orchestra had the composer Max Bruch as its principal conductor for three years?

11 Eric Fenby was the amanuensis of the English composer Frederick Delius. What does this mean?

12 In Frederick Delius's opera *A Village Romeo and Juliet*, the characters take a *Walk to the Paradise Garden*. What exactly was the Paradise Garden?

13 Sir Edward Elgar wrote the music, but who wrote the words to "*Land of Hope and Glory*"?

14 The composers Domenico Scarlatti and George Frideric Handel once had a duel. Handel was on the organ, while Scarlatti played the harpsichord. Who won?

15 The national anthem for which European country is based on music written by Joseph Haydn?

16 Aled Jones became famous for singing "*Walking in the Air*" from *The Snowman*. Who composed the song?

17 The *Can-Can* comes from which operetta by Jacques Offenbach?

18 Henry Purcell was the organist at which English abbey?

19 Benjamin Britten borrowed the theme from Henry Purcell's *Rondo* from *Abdelazar* to use as the basis for his most famous piece for children. What is its name?

20 What was a "Schubertiad"?

Cinematic Sounds

1 Which English composer won an Oscar for his soundtrack to *The Bridge on the River Kwai*?

2 Who wrote the *Organ Symphony* made famous to a whole new generation of listeners by Babe, the pig that thought it was a sheepdog?

3 Oliver Stone notably used which famous piece by Samuel Barber in his Vietnam War film *Platoon*?

4 What is the name of the film which saw the first collaboration between the composer John Williams and the director Stephen Spielberg?

5 What was the name of the Ken Russell film about the life of the English composer Frederick Delius?

6 Who played Gustav Mahler in Ken Russell's 1974 film about the great man?

7 Modest Mussorgky's *Night on a Bare Mountain* was used in which Walt Disney cartoon?

8 The film *Amadeus*, about the life of Wolfgang Amadeus Mozart, was directed by Milos Forman. But upon whose stage play was it based?

9 Joaquín Rodrigo's *Concierto de Aranjuez* was referred to as "Concerto de Orange Juice" in which film about a northern mining town?

10 What was the name of the 1908 film for which Camille Saint-Saëns composed the first ever film soundtrack?

11 Which work by George Frideric Handel was used as the theme music to *The Madness of King George*?

12 Who directed the film *2001: A Space Odyssey*, which used Richard Strauss's *Also sprach Zarathustra* in its opening?

13 The great film composer Erich Korngold became an American citizen in 1943, but what nationality was he originally?

14 For which studio symphony orchestra was Bernard Herrmann the Chief Conductor between 1942 and 1959?

15 From 1924 to 1925, a silent film was produced of one of Richard Strauss's operas, making a significant advance in the relationship between music and cinema in the process. Which opera was it?

16 Which Scottish composer worked with the director Baz Luhrmann on his films *Romeo and Juliet* and *Moulin Rouge*?

17 At which British music college did the composer of the soundtrack to *Titanic*, James Horner, train?

18 What was the name of the 1988 film about the relationship between the cellist Jacqueline du Pré and her sister Hilary?

19 Who composed the music for *Citizen Kane* and *Psycho*?

20 For which film was Arnold Schoenberg's *Accompaniment to a Film Scene* written?

20.

Quick Fire (*Enthusiastic*)

1 What is the name of the style of singing where the composer writes several separate tunes for people with different voices, which combine together harmoniously?

2 Who wrote the 1970 opera, *Taverner*, about the life of the early English composer John Taverner?

3 The composer Thomas Tallis wrote music for two Queens of England. One was Catholic and one was Protestant. Who were they?

4 The early music composer Thomas Tallis was a lay clerk at which English cathedral?

5 With whom did the composer William Byrd operate a job share for around 40 years as the composer and organist to the Chapel Royal?

6 The early music composer William Byrd was the organist and choirmaster at which cathedral between 1563 and 1572?

7 Elizabeth I jointly granted the composers William Byrd and Thomas Tallis a patent allowing them the monopoly on what in England for 21 years from 1575?

8 Jacopo Peri is the man to whom history has given the credit for writing the world's first opera. His first operatic work was called *Dafne*, but what was the name of his second work?

9 For which French king was Jean-Baptiste Lully the personal composer?

10 By the time he was ten, Henry Purcell was a choirboy in which choir?

11 In Purcell's opera *Dido and Aeneas*, Dido is queen of where?

12 What was the first piece of music played on Classic FM?

13 Which work was number one in the first Classic FM Hall of Fame back in 1996?

14 Vivaldi was excused having to say Mass because he claimed to suffer from which illness?

15 Between leaving school and becoming an organist, which instrument did Johann Sebastian Bach make money from playing?

16 Johann Sebastian Bach's first wife, Maria Barbara, was already related to him in what way?

17 When Handel was eight years old a nobleman heard him play and was so impressed that he ensured the boy had lessons. What was his name?

18 At the court of which German nobleman was Handel given a job?

19 "*Zadok the Priest*" was written by George Frideric Handel as a coronation anthem for which English monarch?

20 In which European city was George Frideric Handel's *Messiah* given its premiere in 1741?

2/

True or False?

Decide whether each of these statements is True or False. But be warned; in an attempt to catch you out, some of the details have only been changed very slightly.

1 Ludwig van Beethoven, Franz Schubert and Gustav Mahler each wrote 12 symphonies.
2 Cello is actually short for Violoncello.
3 Every child at school in Belgium is required by law to learn to play the harmonica.
4 Ludwig van Beethoven was the first composer to use a trombone in a symphony.
5 Johann Sebastian Bach wrote a cantata about fizzy water.
6 Johann Sebastian Bach's *Air on the G String* wasn't actually written to be played on a G string at all.
7 The father of film composer John Barry ran a cinema.
8 Ludwig van Beethoven never actually gave the nickname *Moonlight Sonata* to his *Sonata No. 14 in C sharp minor*.
9 Carmen, the heroine in Bizet's eponymous opera, worked in a hosiery factory.
10 Alexander Borodin's first published work was called *On the Action of Ethyl Iodide on Hydrobenzamide and Amarine*.

11 Johannes Brahms used to play piano in brothels as a way of earning his keep.

12 Although Aaron Copland was American, both his parents were originally German.

13 Sir Peter Maxwell Davies wrote his *Farewell to Stromness* to be played as a ship bearing the name "*Stromness*" left port.

14 Claude Debussy finished off his big hit *La Mer* when he was beside the seaside in Bridlington.

15 Antonín Dvořák was a train spotter.

16 George Gershwin once wrote a song called "*I'm a poached egg!*"

17 During the First World War, the French composer Maurice Ravel was a taxi driver.

18 Nikolai Rimsky-Korsakov wrote his *Symphony in E flat* while stationed just off the coast of Bridlington.

19 Charles Darwin was the grandfather of Ralph Vaughan Williams.

20 The film soundtrack composer Hans Zimmer also wrote the theme tune for Henry Kelly's long-running daytime television quiz show, *Going For Gold*.

22

Quick Fire (*Enthusiastic*)

1 Christoph Willibald Gluck's *The Dance of the Blessed Spirits* comes from a ballet section of which of his operas?

2 What is the name of the family who were musical patrons to Joseph Haydn throughout his career?

3 Which member of the Bach family is sometimes referred to as "the London Bach"?

4 How many quintets did Luigi Boccherini compose for various combinations of instruments?

5 During his lifetime, the composer Luigi Boccherini toured Italy, France and Spain as a virtuoso performer on which instrument?

6 By what nickname was Wolfgang Amadeus Mozart's sister Maria Anna known?

7 Wolfgang Amadeus Mozart went on his first tour of Europe when he was six years old. It took in Munich, Vienna, Paris, London and Amsterdam. For how many years did it last?

8 According to legend, upon hearing which popular work in Italy did the young Wolfgang Amadeus Mozart rush off and scribble down the whole work onto manuscript paper, note perfect?

9 What was the name of Wolfgang Amadeus Mozart's wife?

10 How old was Wolfgang Amadeus Mozart when he died?

11 Which operetta composer also wrote the tune to the hymn "*Onward! Christian Soldiers!*"?

12 Which other famous composer did Ludwig van Beethoven describe as being a teacher "from whom I learned absolutely nothing"?

13 Which other famous composer, when he was a boy, played for Wolfgang Amadeus Mozart, impressing the older man enough for him to say: "Keep your eye on him; one day he will make the world talk of him"?

14 What is the composer Louis Spohr said to have invented some time around 1820, for which violinists ever since have had cause to thank him?

15 After he died, why did the church initially refuse to allow the body of Niccolò Paganini to be buried on its land?

16 Franz Schubert contracted syphilis in 1823, but it was another disease that claimed his life five years later. What was it?

17 For which profession did Hector Berlioz begin training in Paris, before switching to music?

18 How many brass bands did Hector Berlioz include in the score for his *Requiem*?

19 A Welsh male voice choir stormed the charts in 2006, with their album becoming the best-selling classical disc of the year. What is their name?

20 Which composer was the first to write a *Ballade* for piano?

The Year in Question

Each of these pairs of events – one musical and one non-musical – took place in the same year in the 1800s and 1900s. But what was the year in question? To help you, the answers are in chronological order.

1 Jacques Offenbach scandalizes polite society in Paris with the first performance of his *Orpheus in the Underworld*, which includes the *Can-Can*. – The Suez Canal Company is formed.

2 Richard Wagner finishes composing his opera *Tristan and Isolde*. – Charles Darwin's *Origin of Species* is published.

3 Frederick Delius is born in England and Claude Debussy is born in France. – Victor Hugo's *Les Misérables* is published.

4 Anton Bruckner finishes his *Mass in D minor* and also his *Symphony Number 0*. – Lewis Carroll's *Alice and Wonderland* and Tolstoy's *War and Peace* are both published.

5 Carl Nielsen is born in Denmark; Alexander Glazunov is born in Russia and Jean Sibelius is born in Finland. – Abraham Lincoln is assassinated.

6 *Coppélia*, a ballet composed by Léo Delibes, gets its premiere in Paris. – Rome is made the capital city of Italy.

7 Richard Wagner's mighty opera cycle *The Ring* receives its first complete performance in Bayreuth. – Alexander Graham Bell invents his telephone.

8 Pyotr Ilyich Tchaikovsky's *Swan Lake* receives its first performance at the Bolshoi Theatre in Moscow. – Thomas Edison invents the phonograph.

9 Antonín Dvořák becomes a star following the publication of his *Slavonic Dances*. – David Hughes invents the microphone.

10 The first, four-volume, edition of George Grove's *Dictionary of Music and Musicians* is published. – Thomas Edison demonstrates a practical incandescent electric light bulb at Menlo Park.

11 The Boston Symphony Orchestra is founded. – Tsar Alexander II is assassinated.

12 The Berlin Philharmonic Orchestra is founded. – Tuberculosis germs are identified by Robert Koch.

13 The Concertgebauw Orchestra is founded in Amsterdam and the Metropolitan Opera is founded in New York. – Robert Louis Stevenson's *Treasure Island* is published.

14 Sergei Rachmaninov finishes composing his *Piano Concerto No. 1*, while he is still a student at the Moscow Conservatoire. – Sir Arthur Conan Doyle's *The Adventures of Sherlock Holmes* is published.

15 Claude Debussy's *Prélude à l'après-midi d'un Faune* is given its first performance in Paris. – Rudyard Kipling's *Jungle Book* is published.

16 Giacomo Puccini's opera *La Bohème* gets its debut in Turin, under the baton of the great Arturo Toscanini. – The first modern Olympic Games take place.

17 George Gershwin is born. – H.G. Wells's *The War of the Worlds* is published.

18 Sir Edward Elgar finishes composing his *Enigma Variations*. – Valdemar Poulsen demonstrates the principle of magnetic tape recording.

19 Birmingham is the venue for the premiere of *The Dream of Gerontius* by Sir Edward Elgar. – Joseph Conrad's *Lord Jim* is published.

20 Giuseppe Verdi dies in Milan. – The first wireless telegraphic signals are sent across the Atlantic by Marconi.

2 4

In Good Voice

All of these singing stars are sopranos, mezzo-sopranos, counter-tenors, tenors, bass-baritones, baritones or basses, but who is which?

1 Roberto Alagna
2 Marcelo Alvarez
3 Cecilia Bartoli
4 Alfie Boe
5 James Bowman
6 Maria Callas
7 José Carreras
8 Plácido Domingo
9 Renée Fleming
10 Lesley Garrett
11 Angela Gheorgiou
12 Katherine Jenkins
13 Emma Kirkby
14 Natasha Marsh
15 Anna Netrebko
16 Anne Sofie von Otter
17 Luciano Pavarotti
18 Andreas Scholl
19 Bryn Terfel
20 John Tomlinson

Quick Fire (*Enthusiastic*)

1 The conductor Hans von Bülow came up with the name "The Three Bs" to describe a trio of composing greats. Who were they?

2 How many strings does a violin have?

3 In the first ten years of the annual listeners' poll, the Classic FM Hall of Fame, which opera consistently achieved the highest position in the chart?

4 Even though he spent 17 years working on it, Alexander Borodin didn't complete his opera *Prince Igor*. Which friend finished it off for him?

5 What subject did Pyotr Ilyich Tchaikovsky study at university?

6 Although there is a school of thought that he deliberately took his own life, what was the official reason given for Pyotr Ilyich Tchaikovsky's death?

7 What is the English translation of Bedřich Smetana's best-known work *Má Vlast*?

8 Of which two forms of transport was Antonín Dvořák a particularly big fan?

9 What were the first two names of W.S. Gilbert (of Gilbert & Sullivan fame)?

10 In which opera by Jacques Offenbach does the *Barcarolle* feature?

11 For which two famous French composers – both of whose names start with the letter "B" – did Léo Delibes work as chorus master at Paris's Théâtre Lyrique?

12 What sort of shop did Edward Elgar's father own during the composer's childhood?

13 What was the name of Giacomo Puccini's final opera?

14 Which of Gustav Mahler's symphonies is known as "The Symphony of a Thousand"?

15 Who said of Sergei Rachmaninov: "[His] immortalizing totality was his scowl. He was a six-and-a-half-foot-tall scowl . . . he was an awesome man"?

16 In which Gloucestershire village was Ralph Vaughan Williams born?

17 At which music college did Ralph Vaughan Williams and Gustav Holst study together?

18 Gustav Holst was of Swedish descent, but in which English county was he born?

19 In an attempt to distract him from composing, Frederick Delius's father sent him to run what sort of business in America?

20 Which two famous composers criss-crossed Hungary, gathering recordings of authentic Hungarian folk tunes on a primitive recording machine which imprinted the sounds on wax cylinders?

26

Mix & Match

Match the famous composer to their big hit:

> ### You can choose from:
>
> *Johann Sebastian Bach; Ludwig van Beethoven; Georges Bizet; George Butterworth; Aaron Copland; Edward Elgar; George Gershwin; George Frideric Handel; Karl Jenkins; Pietro Mascagni; Peter Maxwell Davies; Modest Mussorgsky; Sergei Rachmaninov; Jean Sibelius; Bedřich Smetana; Igor Stravinsky; Pyotr Ilyich Tchaikovsky; Ralph Vaughan Williams; Antonio Vivaldi; William Walton.*

1 *The Lark Ascending*
2 *The Enigma Variations*
3 *The Armed Man (A Mass for Peace)*
4 *Finlandia*
5 *1812 Overture*
6 *Má Vlast*
7 *The Pearl Fishers*
8 *Rhapsody on a Theme of Paganini*
9 *Rhapsody in Blue*
10 *Cavalleria rusticana*

11 *The Four Seasons*
12 *The Banks of Green Willow*
13 *Toccata and Fugue in D minor*
14 *Pictures at an Exhibition*
15 *Egmont overture*
16 *Farewell to Stromness*
17 *Sarabande*
18 *The Rite of Spring*
19 *Crown Imperial*
20 *Appalachian Spring*

Quick Fire (*Enthusiastic*)

1 Which great Russian impresario commissioned Igor Stravinsky to write the ballets *The Firebird* and *Petrushka*?

2 Which fruit was included in the title of an opera by Sergei Prokofiev?

3 In which northern English town was William Walton born?

4 In 1948, William Walton left Britain and moved to which island off the Italian coast?

5 Which of Dmitri Shostakovich's symphonies has the subtitle *"A Soviet Artist's Practical Creative Reply to Just Criticism"*?

6 The American composer John Cage inserted pieces of metal and rubber into the body of a piano to create a variation on the instrument. What was this known as?

7 Benjamin Britten's *War Requiem* was written for the opening of which cathedral?

8 A theme from which work by Henry Purcell features throughout Benjamin Britten's *The Young Person's Guide to the Orchestra*?

9 Of which American orchestra was Leonard Bernstein the music director between 1958 and 1969?

10 Sir Peter Maxwell Davies and Harrison Birtwistle both studied at the Royal Manchester College of Music, along with a group of young British composers. What were they collectively known as?

11 Which soprano featured on a hit recording of Henryk Górecki's *Symphony of Sorrowful Songs* with The London Sinfonietta in the early 1990s?

12 In 1969, Arvo Pärt stopped composing altogether after becoming a member of which religious group?

13 John Tavener's work, *The Protecting Veil*, was written for which cellist?

14 The composers Philip Glass, Steve Reich and Terry Riley are all exponents of a deceptively simple style of music, which often features a few notes repeated over and over again. What is it called?

15 Who was the first composer to be made a life peer?

16 What was the name given to the group of French composers Darius Milhaud, Germaine Tailleferre, Arthur Honegger, Francis Poulenc, Louis Durey and Georges Auric?

17 Where in Oxford was William Walton a boy chorister?

18 Sergei Prokofiev and Dmitri Shostakovich both studied at which Russian music college?

19 In musical circles, what does the acronym FRWCMD stand for?

20 What is the name of the young Russian who took over as the Royal Liverpool Philharmonic Orchestra's Principal Conductor in 2006?

True or False?

Decide whether each of these statements is True or False. But be warned; in an attempt to catch you out, some of the details have only been changed very slightly.

1 The Catholic Church made the nun Hildegard of Bingen a saint.

2 The Italian composer Giovanni Pierluigi da Palestrina's surname wasn't really Palestrina. Palestrina is, in fact, his home town.

3 Pope Marcellus, the dedicatee of Palestrina's *Missa Papae Marcelli*, was dead by the time he'd finished composing it.

4 The Chapel Royal is not actually a place, but is instead a group of singers.

5 Jean-Baptiste Lully made his name in France, but was originally Italian.

6 Georg Philipp Telemann composed around 9,700 works.

7 After he died, it took 46 years to collect and publish all of Johann Sebastian Bach's works.

8 Christoph Willibald Gluck died in Vienna after suffering a series of strokes brought on by his insistence on drinking an after-dinner liqueur against his doctor's wishes.

9 Joseph Haydn very nearly became a castrato, on the advice of his choirmaster, until the boy's father found out and told him what had to happen to him to allow his high voice to remain.

10 By the time he was 12, Wolfgang Amadeus Mozart had already completed seven operas.

11 Edvard Grieg's great-grandfather emigrated to Australia after the Battle of Culloden.

12 As a youngster, the Spanish composer Isaac Albéniz used to perform a party trick where he would stand dressed as a musketeer with the piano keyboard behind him, playing tunes with the backs of his hands.

13 Anton Bruckner graduated from a correspondence course on music composition at the age of 10.

14 *The Four Last Songs* was the last work that Richard Strauss wrote before he died.

15 The composer who wrote *Finlandia* was actually French.

16 When Sergei Rachmaninov moved from Russia to America, he built himself a new home that was absolutely identical to the one he had left behind in Moscow.

17 One of Erik Satie's strangest compositions is called *Vexations*. It is made up of the same few bars of music, which are played over and over again a total of 840 times.

18 Erik Satie's ballet *Parade* features parts for typewriter, whistle, lawnmower, knitting needles and siren.

19 Tortoises, an elephant, kangaroos, donkeys, and gerbils all feature in Camille Saint-Saëns's *Carnival of the Animals*.

20 The chart-topping mezzo-soprano Katherine Jenkins was born in Skegness.

On the Box

Classical music has long been used to help sell all sorts of products in television commercials. Can you match the ten pieces below to the ten products or brands?

> ### You can choose from:
>
> *British Airways; Cadbury Fruit & Nut; De Beers diamonds; Hamlet cigars; Hovis bread; John Lewis; Levi jeans; Lloyds TSB; Old Spice; Orange*

1. Pyotr Ilyich Tchaikovsky: *Dance of the Reed-Flutes* from *The Nutcracker*
2. Carl Orff: "*O Fortuna*" from *Carmina Burana*
3. Karl Jenkins: *Palladio*
4. Léo Delibes: *Flower Duet* from *Lakmé*
5. Johann Sebastian Bach: *Air on a G String*
6. Antonín Dvořák: *Symphony No. 9*
7. George Frideric Handel: *Sarabande*
8. John Tavener: *The Lamb*
9. Elena Kats-Chernin: *Eliza Aria*
10. Einaudi: *Le Onde*

It's not just advertisers who have plundered the classical music back-catalogue for great music. The people who make the programmes between the ad breaks have done the same thing over the years. Match these ten classical works to the ten television programmes to which they provided the signature tune:

You can choose from:

Alfred Hitchcock Presents . . .; The American Civil War; The Eurovision Song Contest; Horse of the Year Show; The Lone Ranger; Monty Python's Flying Circus; The Onedin Line; The Sky at Night; The South Bank Show; What the Papers Say

11 Malcolm Arnold: *English Dance No. 5*
12 Marc-Antoine Charpentier: *Te Deum*
13 Charles Gounod: *Funeral March of a Marionette*
14 Aram Khachaturian: *Adagio of Spartacus and Phrygia*
15 Wolfgang Amadeus Mozart: *A Musical Joke*
16 Sergei Rachmaninov: *Variations on a Theme of Paganini*
17 Gioachino Rossini: *William Tell Overture*
18 John Philip Sousa: *Liberty Bell*

19 Jean Sibelius: *At the Castle Gate* from *Pelléas and Mélisande*
20 Jay Ungar: *The Ashokan Farewell*

Order! Order!

Put these musical instrument formations in the correct order, starting with the one involving the smallest number of musicians:

1	Decimet	6	Quintet
2	Duet	7	Septet
3	Nonet	8	Sextet
4	Octet	9	Solo
5	Quartet	10	Trio

Put these string instruments in order of size, starting with the smallest:

1	Cello	3	Viola
2	Double bass	4	Violin

Put these operas in the order in which they were premiered:

1 Christoph Willibald Gluck: *Orpheus and Eurydice*
2 Claudio Monteverdi: *La Favola d'Orfeo*
3 Georges Bizet: *Carmen*
4 Giacomo Puccini: *Madam Butterfly*
5 Giuseppe Verdi: *Otello*
6 Jacques Offenbach: *Orpheus in the Underworld*

Quick Fire (*Fiendish*)

1 Which is the lowest woodwind instrument of the orchestra?

2 Composer Richard Strauss's father was a horn player who performed a number of premieres for – and was consulted by – which famous German opera composer?

3 It's now virtually disappeared from the musical landscape, but what sort of instrument is a Heckelphone?

4 The jazz saxophonist Jan Garbarek worked with which group of singers on his album *Officium*, which includes the big Classic FM hit *"Parce mihi Domine"*?

5 Which Italian professor pieced together Tomaso Albinoni's *Adagio for Strings* and probably deserves most of the credit for actually writing it?

6 Which fellow famous composer was a torch-bearer at the funeral of Ludwig van Beethoven?

7 What was the name of the Irish actress with whom the French composer Hector Berlioz fell passionately in love, eventually marrying her in 1833?

8 Johannes Brahms wrote his *Academic Festival Overture* when he was given an honorary degree from which university?

9 Anton Bruckner is buried under the organ at a monastery in which city?

10 Frédéric Chopin had a passionate affair with the novelist George Sand. But this was her nom de plume; what was her real name?

11 What is the enigma in Edward Elgar's *Enigma Variations*?

12 Can you name the five composers who together made up "The Mighty Handful"?

13 How many days did Gioachino Rossini claim it took him to write *The Barber of Seville* in its entirety?

14 Camille Saint-Saëns was a clever chap and developed a very keen interest in lepidoptery. What is this the study of?

15 For which orchestra did Jean Sibelius fail his audition as a violinist in 1891?

16 Pyotr Ilyich Tchaikovsky received an honorary degree from Cambridge University in 1893, but there were two other composers there picking up gongs on the same day. Who were they?

17 Name all four members of "The Manchester Group" of composers.

18 What is antiphonal singing?

19 What is the name of the monk who published his theories on musical notation in around 1025, and who is now usually given the credit for inventing the writing down of music?

20 Hildegard of Bingen wasn't really born in Bingen itself. Where was she actually from?

They Come from Where?

Match the famous composers to the country of their birth:

> ### You can choose from:
>
> *Armenia; Austria; Belgium; Canada; England; Estonia; Finland; France; Germany; Hungary; Ireland; Italy; Norway; Poland; Russia; Scotland; Spain; USA; Wales*

1 Frederick Delius
2 Arvo Pärt
3 Zbigniew Preisner
4 Joseph Haydn
5 Louis Spohr
6 Hector Berlioz
7 Franz Liszt
8 Edvard Grieg
9 Isaac Albéniz
10 Arthur Sullivan

11 Jean Sibelius
12 Sergei Rachmaninov
13 George Gershwin
14 Karl Jenkins
15 Howard Shore
16 Aram Khachaturian
17 James MacMillan
18 Patrick Doyle
19 Guillaume Dufay
20 Domenico Zipoli

Name that Composer

Each of the groups of works listed below was written by one person. Can you name that composer?

1 *Holberg Suite; Peer Gynt Suite; Lyric Pieces*
2 *The Mikado; Ivanhoe; Symphony in E*
3 *Lakmé; Coppélia; Sylvia*
4 *By the Beautiful Blue Danube; Tales from the Vienna Woods; Thunder and Lightning Polka*
5 *Aida; La Forza del Destino; La Traviata*
6 *The Flying Dutchman; Lohengrin; Tristan and Isolde*
7 *Academic Festival Overture; Hungarian Dance No. 5; Violin Concerto*
8 *Violin Concerto No. 1 in G minor; Kol Nidrei; Scottish Fantasy*
9 *The Carnival of the Animals; Danse Macabre; "Organ" Symphony No. 3*
10 *Cantique de Jean Racine; Dolly Suite; Clair de Lune*

11 *Enigma Variations; Chanson de Matin; Salut d'Amour*

12 *La Bohème; Gianni Schicchi; Madam Butterfly*

13 *Also sprach Zarathustra; Der Rosenkavalier; Four Last Songs*

14 *Karelia Suite; The Swan of Tuonela; Valse Triste*

15 *Vocalise; Rhapsody on a Theme of Paganini; Aleko*

16 *Clair de Lune; La Mer; Prélude à L'Après-midi d'un Faune*

17 *Le Tombeau de Couperin; Pavane pour une Infante Défunte; Daphnis and Chloé*

18 *Fantasia on a Theme of Thomas Tallis; The Lark Ascending; English Folk Song Suite*

19 *La Calinda; On Hearing the First Cuckoo in Spring; The Walk to the Paradise Garden*

20 *Romeo and Juliet; Lieutenant Kijé Suite; The Love for Three Oranges*

Quick Fire (*Fiendish*)

1 Guillaume de Machaut was one of the "Ars Nova" composers of the 1300s. What does that translate as?
2 Guillaume de Machaut became a canon in which French city around the age of 40?
3 In which cathedral did the Belgian composer Guillaume Dufay begin his career as a boy chorister?
4 The early music composer Thomas Tallis was an organist at which Essex abbey?
5 Elizabeth I granted Thomas Tallis and William Byrd the monopoly on printing music and music paper in 1575. What was their first publication called?
6 Palestrina's *Missa Papae Marcelli* was dedicated to Pope Marcellus. How long did his papacy last?
7 What role did the composer Jacopo Peri take in the first production of his opera *Dafne* in 1598?
8 Where is the composer Orlando Gibbons buried?
9 During the reign of Louis XIV, which composer bought the right to be the only man in France to be allowed to put on operas, staging his first production on a converted tennis court?
10 Which Italian nobleman was responsible for Antonio Vivaldi's works being kept under lock and key, away from public performance, for around two centuries?

11 What was the name of the young soprano with whom the composer Antonio Vivaldi travelled around Europe for many years?

12 When Johann Sebastian Bach's parents died, he was sent to live with his older brother, an organist. What was his name?

13 In 1708, Johann Sebastian Bach was appointed organist to which nobleman?

14 Johann Sebastian Bach married his second wife in 1720. What was her name?

15 Johann Sebastian Bach and George Frideric Handel both suffered from cataracts. The same English surgeon botched operations to cure the problem on both men. What was his name?

16 Which of George Frideric Handel's operas gave him his first smash hit success in London?

17 Domenico Scarlatti is best known for his piano compositions, but his father was a successful composer, too. What was his first name?

18 The Baroque composer Domenico Zipoli was born in Italy, but he emigrated to which continent to work as a Jesuit missionary?

19 The composer Carl Philipp Emanuel Bach worked for which king for some 28 years?

20 Carl Philipp Emanuel Bach was a famous keyboard player who wrote a much respected book on the subject. What was it called?

The Year in Question

Each of these pairs of events – one musical and one non-musical – took place in the same year in the 1900s. But what was the year in question? To help you, the answers are in chronological order.

1 William Walton is born in Oldham. – The United States purchase control of the Panama Canal.

2 The London Symphony Orchestra is founded. – The building of the Panama Canal begins.

3 Franz Léhar's operetta *The Merry Widow* has its first performance in Vienna. – Norway and Sweden become separate countries.

4 Maurice Ravel becomes Ralph Vaughan Williams's teacher in Paris for a three-month period. – Henry Ford produces his first Model T motor car.

5 In Gloucester, Ralph Vaughan Williams conducts the premiere of his *Fantasia on a Theme of Thomas Tallis* for string orchestra. – Dr Crippen becomes the first criminal suspect to be caught by radio when he is arrested on a ship off Canada.

6 Igor Stravinsky's ballet *Petrushka* has its first performance in Paris. – Amundsen arrives at the South Pole.

7 John Cage is born in Los Angeles. – The *Titanic* sinks.

8 Igor Stravinsky's ballet *The Rite of Spring* is given its first performance in Paris, causing something of an outrage. – D.H. Lawrence's *Sons and Lovers* is published.

9 Ralph Vaughan Williams's *London Symphony* has its
first performance. – The First World War breaks out.

10 Sergei Rachmaninov packs his bags, gathers up his
family and abandons his Russian homeland
permanently. – The USA joins the First World War.

11 Leonard Bernstein is born in Massachusetts; Claude
Debussy dies in Paris. – Peace breaks out, following the
end of the First World War.

12 Sir Edward Elgar's *Cello Concerto* is performed for the
first time in London. – Man crosses the Atlantic for the
first time in an aeroplane.

13 The Salzburg Festival opens its doors for the first time.
– The first commercial radio broadcast takes place.

14 He hadn't wanted it to be played during his lifetime, but
Camille Saint-Saëns's *Carnival of the Animals* finally
receives its Paris premiere. – Insulin is discovered.

15 George Gershwin is the star soloist in the New York
premiere of his *Rhapsody in Blue*. – Lenin dies.

16 Giacomo Puccini's opera *Turandot* receives its premiere
in Milan under the baton of Arturo Toscanini. – The
General Strike sweeps across Britain.

17 Sergei Rachmaninov might have been the soloist, but
the premiere performance of his *Piano Concerto No. 4*
in Philadelphia is far from being a crowd pleaser. – The
first television transmission takes place.

18 Ralph Vaughan Williams's *Piano Concerto in C major* is
given its first performance. – FM radio is invented.

19 Sir Edward Elgar and Gustav Holst both die in London; Peter Maxwell Davies is born in Manchester. – The Joliot-Curies announce the creation of an artificial radioactive substance.

20 George Gershwin's opera *Porgy and Bess* is given its first performance in Boston. – T.S. Eliot's play *Murder in the Cathedral* has its first performance.

Mind the Gap

Can you complete these titles, inserting the missing word? To help you along the way, all of the missing words are animals of one sort or another and each asterisk represents a missing letter.

1 Franz Schubert: ***** Quintet in A
2 Frederick Delius: On Hearing the first ****** in Spring
3 Igor Stravinsky: The Fire****
4 Maurice Ravel: Mother ***** Suite
5 Ralph Vaughan Williams: The **** Ascending
6 Gioachino Rossini: The Thieving ******
7 Camille Saint-Saëns: The ****
8 Pyotr Ilyich Tchaikovsky: **** Lake
9 Jean Sibelius: The **** of Tuonela
10 Leos Janáček: The Cunning Little *****
11 Thomas Arne: "Where the *** Sucks"
12 Nikolai Rimsky-Korsakov: The Flight of the *********
13 Giacomo Puccini: Madam *********
14 Ralph Vaughan Williams: The *****
15 Sergei Prokofiev: The Ugly ********
16 Johann Sebastian Bach: "****** May Safely Graze"
17 Modest Mussorgsky: The Song of the ****
18 Sergei Prokofiev: Peter and the ****
19 Camille Saint-Saëns: Carnival of the *******
20 Francis Poulenc: Babar, the little ********

Odd One Out

Which is the odd one out – and why?

1 Mstislav Rostropovich, Evgeny Kissin, Julian Lloyd-Webber, Steven Isserlis, Yo-Yo Ma

2 Glockenspiel, Marimba, Castanets, Cornet, Triangle, Timpani

3 Natalie Clein, Maxim Vengerov, Nicola Benedetti, Joshua Bell, Daniel Hope, Nigel Kennedy

4 Carl Philipp Emmanuel Bach, Johann Christian Bach, Johann Sebastian Bach, Johann Christoph Bach, Wilhelm Friedemann Bach

5 *Sylvia, The Rite of Spring, Swan Lake, Daphnis and Chloé, Petrushka, Carmen*

6 *La Bohème, Carmen, Tosca, Madam Butterfly, Turandot, Gianni Schicchi*

7 *Veritable Flabby Preludes (for a Dog); Sketches and Exasperations of a Big Boob Made of Wood; Five Grins or Mona Lisa's Moustache; Waltz of the Chocolate Almonds; Étude on Consideration of a Striped Ocelot; Things Seen from the Right and Left without Spectacles*

8 *Parsifal, Das Rheingold, Die Walküre, Siegfried, Götterdämmerung*

9 *Star Wars, Rain Man, Raiders of the Lost Ark, Superman, E.T., Harry Potter 1, 2 and 3*

10 Domenico Scarlatti, Johann Sebastian Bach, George Frideric Handel, Domenico Zipoli

11 *The Marriage of Figaro, Turandot, Don Giovanni, Così fan tutte, The Magic Flute*

12 *The Barber of Seville, The Thieving Magpie, William Tell, Otello*

13 George Gershwin, Felix Mendelssohn, Henry Purcell, Camille Saint-Saëns

14 Gustav Mahler, Gaetano Donizetti, Robert Schumann, Bedřich Smetana

15 Alexander Borodin, Mily Balakirev, Nikolai Rimsky-Korsakov, Pyotr Ilyich Tchaikovsky, César Cui, Modest Mussorgsky

16 Domenico Zipoli, Antonín Dvořák, Bedřich Smetana, Josef Suk, Leos Janácek

17 Pablo Martín de Sarasate, Enrique Granados, Manuel de Falla, Isaac Albéniz, Heitor Villa-Lobos

18 *Trial by Jury, The Thieving Magpie, The Pirates of Penzance, HMS Pinafore, The Yeoman of the Guard*

19 Arnold Bax, Hubert Parry, Samuel Coleridge-Taylor, George Butterworth, George Gershwin

20 Emmanuel Chabrier, Charles-Marie Widor, Max Bruch, Joseph Canteloube, Jules Massenet

Quick Fire (*Fiendish*)

1 Wolfgang Amadeus Mozart originally fell in love with his eventual wife's sister. What was her name?

2 Who wrote the 1831 play *Mozart and Salieri*?

3 How many years after Wolfgang Amadeus Mozart was Ludwig van Beethoven born?

4 How old was Ludwig van Beethoven when he died?

5 The composer Louis Spohr was widely respected as a teacher in his day. He wrote a book on the subject that he taught. What was it called?

6 When he was a boy, the German composer Carl Maria von Weber used to travel around the country with his father's company. What sort of company was it?

7 At what age did Gioachino Rossini suddenly stop writing opera altogether, despite penning operatic hit after operatic hit?

8 In 1815, how many songs did Franz Schubert compose?

9 Franz Schubert only ever gave one major concert, in the year of his death, but this event was overshadowed by the arrival of which other famous composer in Vienna at the same time?

10 What job did Hector Berlioz's father do?

11 In what year did the actress Harriet Smithson finally give in and marry Hector Berlioz?

12 Which 20th-century French composer wrote *L'horloge de flore*?

13 How do Americans refer to what we Brits call "crotchets" in musical notation?

14 How many sexual conquests did the servant Leporello claim for his master Don Giovanni in the *"Catalogue Aria"* in Mozart's opera *Don Giovanni*?

15 The great tenor, Enrico Caruso, died at the age of 48. In how many different operas did he sing the leading tenor role at the Metropolitan Opera House in New York during his lifetime?

16 How old was Georges Bizet when he wrote his first symphony?

17 What was the name of Mikhail Glinka's first opera?

18 Modest Mussorgky didn't actually orchestrate much of his opera *Boris Godunov* or his big hit *Night on a Bare Mountain*. Who did it for him?

19 What was the name of the rich widow who funded Pyotr Ilyich Tchaikovsky's work on the condition that they should never meet?

20 *Vltava* is the most popular section of Bedřich Smetana's *Má Vlast*. How many other sections are there?

Mix & Match

Match these composers to their musical eras:

> ## You can choose from:
>
> *Early; Baroque; Classical; Romantic; Modern*

1   Johann Sebastian Bach
2   Leonard Bernstein
3   Georges Bizet
4   Benjamin Britten
5   Anton Bruckner
6   John Cage
7   Léo Delibes
8   Karl Ditters von Dittersdorf
9   Guillaume Dufay
10 John Dunstable
11 Gustav Mahler
12 Johann Pachelbel
13 Niccolò Paganini
14 John Rutter
15 Robert Schumann
16 Arthur Sullivan
17 Thomas Tallis
18 John Tavener
19 Antonio Vivaldi
20 Carl Maria von Weber

Order! Order!

Put these composers in the order of their birth:

1 César Franck
2 Claudio Monteverdi
3 Dmitri Shostakovich
4 Edvard Grieg
5 Edward Elgar
6 Felix Mendelssohn
7 Joseph Haydn
8 George Gershwin
9 Henry Purcell
10 Hildegard of Bingen
11 Igor Stravinsky
12 Johann Sebastian Bach
13 Johann Strauss Sr
14 Jules Massenet
15 Ludwig van Beethoven
16 Max Bruch
17 Patrick Hawes
18 Philip Glass
19 Samuel Barber
20 Wolfgang Amadeus Mozart

Quick Fire (*Fiendish*)

1 What big job in New York did Antonín Dvořák hold in the 1890s?

2 How many years separate the birthdays of Johann Strauss Sr and Johann Strauss Jr?

3 To what philanthropic enterprise did Giuseppe Verdi bequeath his considerable riches?

4 How many years after Johannes Brahms was Max Bruch born?

5 Which other famous French composer took over from Camille Saint-Saëns as organist at the church of La Madeleine in Paris?

6 In what sort of office did Edward Elgar work as a young man, before turning to music full-time?

7 In Edward Elgar's *Enigma Variations*, what was the name of the person upon whom *Nimrod* was based?

8 Who conducted the premiere of Giacomo Puccini's opera *Turandot*?

9 In 1897, Gustav Mahler became the conductor of which great opera company?

10 What was the name of Sergei Rachmaninov's first opera, which he wrote when he was just 19 years old?

11 What mark did Pyotr Ilyich Tchaikovsky give to Sergei Rachmaninov when the latter played for him at the Moscow Conservatory?

12 What was the name of the hypnotist to whom Sergei Rachmaninov dedicated his *Piano Concerto No. 2*?

13 Which was Gustav Holst's main instrument as a player?

14 While Frederick Delius was living in America, he took lessons from which American organist?

15 What was the name of Frederick Delius's amanuensis?

16 Which 20th-century composer is credited with inventing "serialism"?

17 For which orchestra did Béla Bartók compose his *Concerto for Orchestra*?

18 Aaron Copland changed his surname. What was it originally?

19 In 1934, Stalin stormed out of a performance of an opera by Dmitri Shostakovich, which resulted in the composer being branded "an enemy of the people". What was the name of the opera?

20 Benjamin Britten was born in which Suffolk town?

Mix & Match

Match the list of first names to the surname of each of the composers:

> ### You can choose from:
>
> *Albéniz; Allegri; Berlioz; Brahms; Delius; Gibbons; Glinka; Górecki; Liszt; McCartney; Mussorgsky; Offenbach; Peri; Ravel; Rimsky-Korsakov; Salieri; Schoenberg; Smetana; Spohr; Vaughan Williams*

1 Antonio
2 Arnold
3 Bedřich
4 Franz
5 Frederick
6 Gregorio
7 Hector
8 Henryk
9 Isaac
10 Jacopo

11 Jacques
12 Johannes
13 Louis
14 Maurice
15 Mikhail
16 Modest
17 Nikolai
18 Orlando
19 Paul
20 Ralph

Whose Aria is it Anyway?

From which opera is each aria or chorus taken?

1 *"Che gelida manina"*
2 *"Brindisi"*
3 *Anvil Chorus*
4 *Lensky's Aria*
5 *"Va pensiero"*
6 *"Where e'er you walk"*
7 *"Mon coeur s'ouvre à ta voix"*
8 *"La donna è mobile"*
9 *"Summertime"*
10 *"E lucevan le stelle"*
11 *Champagne Aria*
12 *"Una furtiva lagrima"*
13 *"Che farò senza Euridice"*
14 *"Der Vogelfänger bin ich ja"*
15 *"Chi il bel sogno"*
16 *"Bella figlia"*
17 *"Dove sono"*
18 *The Catalogue Aria*
19 *Habanera*
20 *Humming Chorus*

Cinematic Sounds

Match the classical work to the film in which it featured:

You can choose from:

2001: A Space Odyssey; A Beautiful Mind; A Clockwork Orange; A Room with a View; Apocalypse Now; Babe; Bend it Like Beckham; Billy Elliot; Brassed Off; Bridget Jones's Diary; The Ladykillers; Natural Born Killers; Out of Africa; Platoon; Pretty Woman; The Shawshank Redemption; Shine; The Silence of the Lambs; Trainspotting; What's Opera, Doc?

1 Johann Sebastian Bach: *Goldberg Variations*
2 Samuel Barber: *Adagio for Strings*
3 Ludwig van Beethoven: *Symphony No. 9*

4 Georges Bizet: *Habanera* from *Carmen*

5 Luigi Boccherini: *Minuet*

6 George Frideric Handel: *"Hallelujah Chorus"* from *Messiah*

7 Wolfgang Amadeus Mozart: *Clarinet Concerto*

8 Wolfgang Amadeus Mozart: *"Che soave zeffiretto"* from *The Marriage of Figaro*

9 Wolfgang Amadeus Mozart: *Piano Sonata No. 11*

10 Carl Orff: *Carmina Burana*

11 Giacomo Puccini: *Doretta's Dream* from *La Rondine*

12 Giacomo Puccini: *"Nessun dorma"* from *Turandot*

13 Sergei Rachmaninov: *Piano Concerto No. 3*

14 Joaquín Rodrigo: *Concierto de Aranjuez*

15 Camille Saint-Saëns: *Organ Symphony No. 3*

16 Richard Strauss: *Also sprach Zarathustra*

17 Pyotr Ilyich Tchaikovsky: *Swan Lake*

18 Antonio Vivaldi: *Four Seasons*

19 Richard Wagner: *Tannhäuser*

20 Richard Wagner: *Ride of the Valkyries*

Operatic Dons

1 In which opera by Gaetano Donizetti did Don Alfonso appear?

2 In which opera by Wolfgang Amadeus Mozart did Don Alfonso appear?

3 In which operetta by W.S. Gilbert and Arthur Sullivan did Don Alhambra del Bolero appear?

4 In which opera by Gioachino Rossini did Don Alonzo appear?

5 In which opera by Jean-Philippe Rameau did Don Alvar appear?

6 In which opera by Giuseppe Verdi did Don Alvaro appear?

7 In which opera by Wolfgang Amadeus Mozart did Don Basilio appear?

8 In which opera by Gioachino Rossini did Don Basilio appear?

9 In which opera by Jean-Philippe Rameau did Don Carlos appear?

10 In which opera by Wolfgang Amadeus Mozart did Don Cassandro appear?

11 In which opera by Wolfgang Amadeus Mozart did Don Curzio appear?

12 In which opera by Ludwig van Beethoven did Don Fernando appear?

13 In which opera by Wolfgang Amadeus Mozart did Don Giovanni appear?

14 In which opera by Georges Bizet did Don José appear?

15 In which opera by Frederick Delius did Don José Martinez appear?

16 In which opera by Wolfgang Amadeus Mozart did Don Ottavio appear?

17 In which opera by Ludwig van Beethoven did Don Pizaro appear?

18 In which opera by Wolfgang Amadeus Mozart did Don Polidoro appear?

19 In which opera by Henry Purcell did Don Quixote appear?

20 Don Carlo appeared in three operas by Giuseppe Verdi. Can you name one of them?

Mix & Match

Match the following famous Christmas carol tunes to their composers:

You can choose from:

Benjamin Britten; Victor Hely-Hutchinson; Gustav Holst; Felix Mendelssohn; Ralph Vaughan-Williams

1 "Hark the Herald Angels Sing"
2 "See Amid the Winter's Snow"
3 *Ceremony of Carols*
4 *Fantasia on Christmas Carols*
5 *A Carol Symphony*

Match the dates to each of the classical music eras:

You can choose from:

Baroque; Classical; Early; Modern; Romantic

1 Before 1600
2 1600–1750
3 1750–1830
4 1830–1900
5 1900–today

The Planets Suite is Gustav Holst's best-known work. Can you match the planets with their astrological influences?

You can choose from:

Jollity; Magic; Old Age; Mysticism; Peace; War

1 Mars
2 Venus
3 Jupiter
4 Uranus
5 Saturn
6 Neptune

The Year in Question

Each of these pairs of events – one musical and one non-musical – took place in the same year in the 1900s. But what was the year in question? To help you, the answers are in chronological order.

1 Sergei Prokofiev's *Peter and the Wolf* is given its premiere in Moscow. – The Spanish Civil War breaks out.

2 Samuel Barber's *Adagio for Strings* is performed for the first time in New York. – The uranium atom is split for the first time.

3 Aaron Copland's ballet *Rodeo* is given its first performance in New York. – The Battle of El Alamein takes place.

4 The Edinburgh International Festival opens. – India becomes independent.

5 Benjamin Britten's Aldeburgh Festival opens. – The state of Israel is founded.

6 Ralph Vaughan Williams's *Sinfonia Antarctica* is given its debut in Manchester. – Mount Everest is conquered for the first time.

7 Ralph Vaughan Williams dies. – Krushchev becomes leader of Russia and De Gaulle becomes leader of France.

8 Benjamin Britten's *War Requiem* is performed for the first time, in the newly rebuilt Coventy Cathedral. – The Berlin Wall is built.

9 Igor Stravinksy dies in New York. – War breaks out between India and Pakistan.

10 Peter Maxwell Davies's opera *Taverner* is given its premiere at the Royal Opera House in London's Covent Garden. – Britain imposes direct rule on Northern Ireland.

11 Dmitri Shostakovich dies in Moscow. – The Vietnam War ends.

12 Philip Glass composes his opera *Einstein on the Beach*. – Mao Tse-tung dies.

13 The film *Out of Africa*, with score by John Barry, is released. – Mikhail Gorbachev becomes leader of the Soviet Union.

14 John Adams finishes his opera *Nixon in China*. – *The Herald of Free Enterprise* capsizes off Zeebrugge.

15 The towering German conductor Herbert von Karajan dies. – The Tiananmen Square massacre takes place in China.

16 The first Three Tenors Concert takes place at the World Cup Final in Rome. – Iraq invades Kuwait.

17 Classic FM begins broadcasting classical music across the UK. – Bill Clinton becomes President of the USA.

18 The Henry Wood Promenade Concerts are 100 years old. – The Channel Tunnel opens.

19 One of the greatest opera houses anywhere in the world, Teatro La Fenice in Venice, is ravaged by fire. – The former French President, François Mitterrand, dies.

20 The violinist and conductor Yehudi Menuhin dies. – The Euro is launched across most of Europe, but not in the UK.

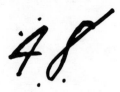

Order! Order!

Put these musical note values in the correct order, starting with the note that lasts for the longest number of beats:

1 Breve
2 Crotchet
3 Demisemiquaver
4 Hemidemisemiquaver
5 Minim
6 Quaver
7 Semibreve
8 Semiquaver

Put the operas that make up Wagner's *Ring* Cycle in their correct order of performance:

1 *Das Rheingold*
2 *Die Walküre*
3 *Götterdämmerung*
4 *Siegfried*

The composer Igor Stravinsky liked to move around. Put the following countries in the order in which he lived in them:

1 France
2 Russia
3 Switzerland
4 USA

Put the following ballets in the order in which they were written:

1 Adolphe Adam: *Giselle*
2 Léo Delibes: *Coppélia*
3 Igor Stravinsky: *Pulcinella*
4 Pyotr Ilyich Tchaikovsky: *The Sleeping Beauty*

49

Name that Composer

Each of the groups of works listed below was written by one person. Can you name that composer?

1 *Gloria; The Story of Babar, the Little Elephant; Organ Concerto*

2 *Rhapsody in Blue; Porgy and Bess; An American in Paris*

3 *Fanfare for the Common Man; Rodeo; Appalachian Spring*

4 *Spitfire Prelude and Fugue; Crown Imperial; Orb and Sceptre*

5 *Jazz Suites; The Assault on Beautiful Gorky; The Gadfly*

6 *The Young Person's Guide to the Orchestra; Peter Grimes; Ceremony of Carols*

7 *Candide; Chichester Psalms; West Side Story*

8 *Spiegel im Spiegel; Cantus Memoriam Benjamin Britten; Tabula Rasa*

9 *The Protecting Veil; The Lamb; Song for Athene*

10 *Koyaanisqatsi; The Hours; Kundun*

11 *A Gaelic Blessing; For the Beauty of the Earth; The Candlelight Carol*

12 *Adiemus: Songs of Sanctuary; Palladio; The Armed Man: A Mass for Peace*

13 *Liverpool Oratorio; Standing Stone; "Ecce Cor Meum"*

14 *Le Onde; Eden Roc; I Giorni*

15 *The Dying Swan; The Hitchhiker's Guide to the Galaxy; Once Around the Sun*

16 *Star Wars; Harry Potter 1, 2 and 3; Schindler's List*

17 *Out of Africa; Dances with Wolves; The Beyondness of Things*

18 *Gangs of New York; The Silence of the Lambs; The Lord of the Rings*

19 *Braveheart; Titanic; A Beautiful Mind*

20 *Gladiator; Mission Impossible; My Beautiful Laundrette*

Heavenly Music

Match each of the composers to their star sign:

> ## You can choose from:
>
> *Aquarius; Pisces; Aries; Taurus; Gemini; Cancer; Leo; Virgo; Libra; Scorpio; Sagittarius; Capricorn*

1 Ludwig van Beethoven
2 Hector Berlioz
3 Johannes Brahms
4 Max Bruch
5 Aaron Copland
6 Claude Debussy
7 Frederick Delius
8 Léo Delibes
9 Edward Elgar
10 George Gershwin

11 Alexander Glazunov
12 Christoph Willibald Gluck
13 Edvard Greig
14 George Frideric Handel
15 Joseph Haydn
16 Gustav Holst
17 Gustav Mahler
18 Wolfgang Amadeus Mozart
19 Johann Pachelbel
20 Giacomo Puccini
21 Johann Strauss Jr
22 Sergei Rachmaninov
23 Dmitri Shostakovich
24 Pyotr Ilyich Tchaikovsky

The Answers

You will find all of the answers to the 1,000 questions asked over the past 100 or so pages in this next section of our book. Keep your score for each of the 50 rounds as you work your way through the book, and then add them all up to give yourself a grand total score out of 1,000 at the end.

Quick Fire (*Friendly*)

Score /20

1 Play with a spikier sound, detaching the notes from each other
2 Works
3 Russia over France
4 Overture
5 Luciano Pavarotti, Plácido Domingo and José Carreras
6 James Galway
7 Quiet Loud
8 Tuba
9 Stephen Sondheim
10 Aldeburgh
11 Sir Peter Maxwell Davies
12 Adam Smith
13 Goretski
14 104
15 Soft Machine
16 Brother and sister
17 *Piano Concerto No. 2.* They were published in the wrong order.
18 *Boléro*
19 Foie gras and truffles
20 Cambridge

02

Cinematic Sounds

Score /20

1 *Dangerous Moonlight*
2 *Dances with Wolves*
3 *The Magnificent Seven*
4 *The Snowman*
5 *The Heiress*
6 *Pride and Prejudice*
7 *Sense and Sensibility*
8 *The Hours*
9 *Alien*
10 *Titanic*
11 *Robin Hood, Prince of Thieves*
12 *The Mission*
13 *The Piano*
14 *Lieutenant Kijé*
15 *The Gadfly*
16 *The Lord of the Rings*
17 *49th Parallel*
18 *Henry V*
19 *Superman*
20 *Gladiator*

Quick Fire (*Friendly*)

Score /20

1 *Symphony No. 8*
2 She was a famous concert pianist and she composed as well
3 Johann Strauss Sr
4 Johann Strauss Jr
5 The Divine Comedy
6 The Red Priest
7 John Taverner was born first
8 Pope Gregory I
9 Hildegard of Bingen
10 Re-birth
11 Karl Jenkins
12 Thomas Cromwell
13 Work
14 The Vatican
15 He speared his foot with his conducting baton, dying of gangrene two months later
16 *Te Deum*
17 Concerto Grosso
18 They are all *Canons* (sometimes referred to as rounds)
19 *"When I am laid in earth"*
20 EMI Classics

04

The Year in Question

Score	/20
1	1703
2	1711
3	1717
4	1720
5	1724
6	1727
7	1727
8	1736
9	1739
10	1740
11	1742
12	1752
13	1756
14	1759
15	1770
16	1782
17	1786
18	1794
19	1797
20	1799

Order! Order!

Score /20

1 Catherina Dorothea (1708)
2 Wilhelm Friedemann (1710)
3 Maria Sophia (1713)
4 Johann Christoph (1713)
5 Carl Philipp Emanuel (1714)
6 Johann Gottfried Bernhard (1715)
7 Leopold August (1718)
8 Christiane Sophie Henriette (1723)
9 Gottfried Heinrich (1724)
10 Christian Gottlieb (1725)
11 Elisabeth Juliane Friederike (1726)
12 Ernst Andreas (1727)
13 Regine Johanna (1728)
14 Christiana Benedicta (1730)
15 Christiana Dorothea (1731)
16 Johann Christoph Friedrich (1732)
17 Johann August Abraham (1733)
18 Johann Christian (1735)
19 Johanna Carolina (1737)
20 Regine Susanna (1742)

Quick Fire (*Friendly*)

Score **/20**

1 St John and St Matthew
2 He added up the alphabetical position of each of the component letters of his surname
3 The attic of their home
4 King George I
5 Westminster Abbey
6 Dittersdorf
7 Prince Archbishop of Salzburg
8 Antonio Salieri
9 Vienna
10 Lesley Garrett
11 Ralph Vaughan Williams
12 Holland
13 *Fidelio*
14 Romantic
15 Navy
16 *The Arabian Nights*
17 Czech
18 A carpet
19 Liverpool
20 Worcestershire

True or False

Score /20

1 True
2 True
3 True
4 True
5 True
6 True
7 True
8 False – a piccolo is smaller than a flute
9 False – a sackbut is an early version of a trombone
10 False – he retired 60 years earlier, in 1913
11 True
12 False – he is a pianist
13 False – he did visit Scotland
14 False – he's famous for his works for piano
15 True
16 True
17 True
18 True
19 True
20 False – he lived to the age of 70, having earned considerable riches along the way

Quick Fire (*Friendly*)

Score **/20**

1 *Enigma Variations*
2 *"None shall sleep"*
3 Sting
4 Eastbourne
5 Ralph was pronounced "Rafe" to rhyme with "safe". Any word that rhymes with this is correct.
6 Sergei Rachmaninov's *Piano Concerto No. 2*
7 St Paul's School for Girls in London
8 Bradford
9 There was a riot among members of the audience
10 Stalin
11 Rhône-Poulenc
12 *Porgy and Bess*
13 Edith Sitwell
14 Yuri Gagarin
15 *4'33"*
16 Ringo Starr
17 Liverpool's Anglican cathedral
18 *"Ecce Cor Meum"*
19 *Pure*
20 Car mechanic

09

Birthday Bonanza

Score /20

1 Marc-Antoine Charpentier
2 Georg Philipp Telemann
3 George Frideric Handel
4 Carl Philipp Emanuel Bach
5 Johann Christian Bach
6 Karl Ditters von Dittersdorf
7 Gioachino Rossini
8 Mikhail Glinka
9 Richard Wagner
10 Johann Strauss Jr
11 Alexander Borodin
12 Camille Saint-Saëns
13 Georges Bizet
14 Sergei Rachmaninov
15 Béla Bartók
16 Joaquín Rodrigo
17 John Barry
18 Karl Jenkins
19 Howard Shore
20 Joby Talbot

They Said What?

Score /20

1 Johann Sebastian Bach
2 Arnold Bax
3 Ludwig van Beethoven
4 Hector Berlioz
5 Leonard Bernstein
6 Johannes Brahms
7 Benjamin Britten
8 Aaron Copland
9 Gustav Holst
10 Pietro Mascagni
11 Wolfgang Amadeus Mozart
12 Nicolò Paganini
13 Sergei Rachmaninov
14 Maurice Ravel
15 Gioachino Rossini
16 Robert Schumann
17 Jean Sibelius
18 Richard Strauss
19 Igor Stravinsky
20 Pyotr Ilyich Tchaikovsky

Mix & Match

Score /20

1 The Philosopher
2 Lamentation
3 Mercury
4 Farewell
5 Maria Theresa
6 The Passion
7 The Schoolmaster
8 Fire
9 The Distracted
10 The Hunt
11 The Bear
12 The Hen
13 The Queen
14 Oxford
15 Surprise
16 Miracle
17 Military
18 Clock
19 Drum Roll
20 London

/2

Order! Order!

Score   /20

Musical Speeds:

1 Largo
2 Adagio
3 Andante
4 Allegretto
5 Allegro
6 Presto

Voices:

1 Soprano
2 Mezzo-soprano
3 Tenor
4 Baritone
5 Bass-baritone
6 Bass

Masters of the King's/Queen's Music:

1 Nicholas Lanier (1625)
2 William Boyce (1755)
3 Edward Elgar (1924)
4 Arnold Bax (1942)
5 Arthur Bliss (1953)
6 Peter Maxwell Davies (2004)

Mozart's Names

1 Johannes
2 Chrysostomus
3 Wolfgangus
4 Amadeus

Mix & Match

Score   /20

1 London
2 Liverpool
3 Amsterdam
4 New York
5 Los Angeles
6 Edinburgh
7 Gateshead
8 Poole
9 Cardiff
10 Manchester
11 Birmingham
12 Vienna
13 Basingstoke
14 Belfast
15 Aldeburgh
16 Leipzig
17 Zürich
18 Croydon
19 Washington
20 Glasgow

14

The Year in Question

Score /20

1 1800
2 1811
3 1813
4 1814
5 1815
6 1819
7 1823
8 1833
9 1836
10 1838
11 1840
12 1842
13 1844
14 1845
15 1846
16 1847
17 1848
18 1849
19 1853
20 1854

Whose Aria is it Anyway?

Score /20

1 Giuseppe Verdi: *Aida*
2 Gioachino Rossini: *The Barber of Seville*
3 Giacomo Puccini: *La Bohème*
4 Georges Bizet: *Carmen*
5 Léo Delibes: *Lakmé*
6 Wolfgang Amadeus Mozart: *The Marriage of Figaro*
7 Giuseppe Verdi: *Nabucco*
8 Georges Bizet: *The Pearl Fishers*
9 Henry Purcell: *Dido and Aeneas*
10 Giuseppe Verdi: *La Traviata*
11 Giuseppe Verdi: *Otello*
12 Antonín Dvořák: *Rusalka*
13 Vincenzo Bellini: *Norma*
14 Giacomo Puccini: *Turandot*
15 Wolfgang Amadeus Mozart: *Don Giovanni*
16 Ludwig van Beethoven: *Fidelio*
17 Giacomo Puccini: *Gianni Schicchi*
18 Pietro Mascagni: *Cavalleria Rusticana*
19 Giacomo Puccini: *Tosca*
20 George Gershwin: *Porgy and Bess*

Definitive Mix & Match

Score /20

1 trio
2 oratorio
3 a capella
4 quintet
5 allegro
6 toccata
7 aria
8 chamber music
9 concerto
10 gavotte
11 legato
12 libretto
13 Kapellmeister
14 quartet
15 movement
16 intermezzo
17 adagio
18 opus
19 cadenza
20 Lieder

Name that Composer

Score /20

1 Henry Purcell
2 Antonio Vivaldi
3 Johann Sebastian Bach
4 George Frideric Handel
5 Franz Joseph Haydn
6 Wolfgang Amadeus Mozart
7 Ludwig van Beethoven
8 Franz Schubert
9 Hector Berlioz
10 Felix Mendelssohn
11 Frédéric Chopin
12 Robert Schumann
13 Franz Liszt
14 Georges Bizet
15 Mikhail Glinka
16 Alexander Borodin
17 Modest Mussorgsky
18 Nikolai Rimsky-Korsakov
19 Pyotr Ilyich Tchaikovsky
20 Antonín Dvořák

Quick Fire (*Enthusiastic*)

Score /20

1 Elephant
2 Francis Poulenc
3 Ibsen
4 John Field
5 English horn
6 London Symphony Orchestra
7 Catrin Finch
8 Adolphe Sax
9 Dietrich Buxtehude
10 Royal Liverpool Philharmonic Orchestra
11 He wrote out Delius's music when the composer was too ill to do it himself
12 A pub
13 A.C. Benson
14 Neither. Handel was declared the victor on the organ and Scarlatti the victor on the harpsichord.
15 Germany
16 Howard Blake
17 *Orpheus in the Underworld*
18 Westminster Abbey
19 *The Young Person's Guide to the Orchestra*
20 A musical party thrown by Franz Schubert

Cinematic Sounds

Score   /20

1 Sir Malcolm Arnold
2 Camille Saint-Saëns
3 *Adagio for Strings*
4 *The Sugarland Express*
5 *A Song of Summer*
6 Robert Powell
7 *Fantasia*
8 Peter Schaffer
9 *Brassed Off*
10 *L'assassinat du Duc de Guise*
11 *Zadok the Priest*
12 Stanley Kubrick
13 Austrian
14 CBS Symphony Orchestra
15 *Der Rosenkavalier*
16 Craig Armstrong
17 Royal College of Music in London
18 *Hilary and Jackie*
19 Bernard Herrmann
20 It wasn't written for any particular film or scene

20.

Quick Fire (*Enthusiastic*)

Score /20

1 Polyphony
2 Sir Peter Maxwell Davies
3 Mary I and Elizabeth I
4 Canterbury Cathedral
5 Thomas Tallis
6 Lincoln Cathedral
7 Printing music and music paper
8 *Euridice*
9 King Louis XIV
10 The Chapel Royal
11 Carthage
12 *Zadok the Priest*
13 Max Bruch's *Violin Concerto No. 1*
14 Asthma
15 Violin
16 They were cousins
17 The Duke of Saxe-Weissenfels
18 The Elector of Hanover
19 King George II
20 Dublin

2/

True or False?

Score /20

1 False – they each wrote nine
2 True
3 True
4 True – in his *Symphony No. 5*
5 False – he did write one about coffee, though
6 True
7 True
8 True
9 False – she worked in a cigarette factory
10 True
11 True
12 False – his parents were originally Russian
13 False – it was a protest against a nuclear reprocessing plant
14 False – he was in Eastbourne
15 True
16 True
17 False – he was an ambulance driver
18 False – he was off the coast of Gravesend
19 False – Darwin was his great-uncle
20 True

22

Quick Fire (*Enthusiastic*)

Score /20

1 *Orpheus and Euridice*
2 Esterházy
3 Johann Christian Bach
4 154
5 Cello
6 Nannerl
7 4 years
8 Allegri's *Miserere*
9 Constanze Weber
10 35
11 Arthur Sullivan
12 Joseph Haydn
13 Ludwig van Beethoven
14 The chin rest for the violin
15 Because it was widely believed at the time that he had made a pact with the devil
16 Typhus
17 He started to train to be a doctor
18 Four – one on each corner of the stage
19 Fron Male Voice Choir
20 Frédéric Chopin

23

The Year in Question

Score /20

1 1858
2 1859
3 1862
4 1864
5 1865
6 1870
7 1876
8 1877
9 1878
10 1879
11 1881
12 1882
13 1883
14 1891
15 1894
16 1896
17 1898
18 1899
19 1900
20 1901

24

In Good Voice

Score **/20**

1 Tenor
2 Tenor
3 Mezzo-soprano
4 Tenor
5 Counter-tenor)
6 Soprano
7 Tenor
8 Tenor
9 Soprano
10 Soprano
11 Soprano
12 Mezzo-soprano
13 Soprano
14 Soprano
15 Soprano
16 Mezzo-soprano
17 Tenor
18 Counter-tenor
19 Bass-baritone
20 Bass

Quick Fire (*Enthusiastic*)

Score /20

1 Johann Sebastian Bach, Ludwig van Beethoven, Johannes Brahms
2 Four
3 Georges Bizet's *The Pearl Fishers*
4 Nikolai Rimsky-Korsakov
5 Law
6 He was poisoned by drinking water infected by cholera
7 *My Homeland*
8 Trains and ships
9 William Schwenck
10 *The Tales of Hoffman*
11 Hector Berlioz and Georges Bizet
12 A music shop
13 *Turandot*
14 *Symphony No. 8*
15 Igor Stravinsky
16 Down Ampney
17 The Royal College of Music
18 Gloucestershire
19 An orange plantation
20 Béla Bartók and Zoltán Kodály

26

Mix & Match

Score /20

1 Ralph Vaughan Williams
2 Edward Elgar
3 Karl Jenkins
4 Jean Sibelius
5 Pyotr Ilyich Tchaikovsky
6 Bedřich Smetana
7 Georges Bizet
8 Sergei Rachmaninov
9 George Gershwin
10 Pietro Mascagni
11 Antonio Vivaldi
12 George Butterworth
13 Johann Sebastian Bach
14 Modest Mussorgsky
15 Ludwig van Beethoven
16 Peter Maxwell Davies
17 George Frideric Handel
18 Igor Stravinsky
19 William Walton
20 Aaron Copland

Quick Fire (*Enthusiastic*)

Score /20

1 Sergei Diaghilev
2 Oranges – in his opera *The Love for Three Oranges*
3 Oldham
4 Ischia
5 *Symphony No. 5*
6 A prepared piano
7 Coventry Cathedral
8 *Abdelazar*
9 New York Philharmonic Orchestra
10 The Manchester School
11 Dawn Upshaw
12 Russian Orthodox Church
13 Steven Isserlis
14 Minimalism
15 Benjamin Britten
16 Les Six
17 Christ Church Cathedral, Oxford
18 St Peterburg Conservatory
19 Fellow of the Royal Welsh College of Music and Drama
20 Vasily Petrenko

True or False?

Score /20

1 False – she was only considered for canonisation

2 True

3 True

4 True

5 True

6 False – he was prolific, but not that prolific, composing 3,700 works during his lifetime

7 True

8 True

9 True

10 False – he had written two operas by the age of 12

11 False – he emigrated to Scandinavia

12 True

13 False – he didn't graduate from a correspondence course in composition until he was 37

14 False – they were separate songs written over a two-year period which were brought together and published after his death

15 False – Jean Sibelius was Finnish

16 True

17 True

18 False – we made up the bit about the lawnmower and the knitting needles. The other three "instruments" are true, though!

19 False – there are no gerbils in the work

20 False – she was born in the Welsh town of Neath

29

On The Box

Score /20

1 Cadbury Fruit & Nut
2 Old Spice
3 De Beers diamonds
4 British Airways
5 Hamlet cigars
6 Hovis bread
7 Levi jeans
8 Orange
9 Lloyds TSB
10 John Lewis
11 What the Papers Say
12 Eurovision Song Contest
13 Alfred Hitchcock Presents . . .
14 The Onedin Line
15 Horse of the Year Show
16 The South Bank Show
17 The Lone Ranger
18 Monty Python's Flying Circus
19 The Sky at Night
20 The American Civil War

Order! Order!

Score **/20**

Musical Instrument Formations

1 Solo
2 Duet
3 Trio
4 Quartet
5 Quintet
6 Sextet
7 Septet
8 Octet
9 Nonet
10 Decimet

Stringed Instruments

1 Violin
2 Viola
3 Cello
4 Double bass

Operas

1 Claudio Monteverdi: *La Favola d'Orfeo*
2 Christoph Willibald Gluck: *Orpheus and Eurydice*
3 Jacques Offenbach: *Orpheus in the Underworld*
4 Georges Bizet: *Carmen*
5 Giuseppe Verdi: *Otello*
6 Giacomo Puccini: *Madam Butterfly*

Quick Fire (*Fiendish*)

Score /20

1 Bassoon
2 Richard Wagner
3 Oboe
4 The Hilliard Ensemble
5 Remo Giazotto
6 Franz Schubert
7 Harriet Smithson
8 University of Bremen
9 Vienna
10 Amandine-Aurore-Lucile Dupin
11 Nobody's really sure. He took it with him to the grave – but we hope that you had fun guessing
12 Alexander Borodin, Modest Mussorgsky, Mily Balakirev, César Cui and Nikolai Rimsky-Korsakov
13 Thirteen
14 Butterflies
15 Vienna Philharmonic Orchestra
16 Camille Saint-Saëns and Max Bruch
17 Peter Maxwell Davies, Harrison Birtwistle, John Ogdon and Elgar Haworth
18 A type of unaccompanied church singing where two parts of a choir sing alternately, with the second section answering the first
19 Guido d'Arezzo
20 Bemersheim, near Alzey in Germany

They Come from Where?

Score **/20**

1 England
2 Estonia
3 Poland
4 Austria
5 Germany
6 France
7 Hungary
8 Norway
9 Spain
10 England
11 Finland
12 Russia
13 USA
14 Wales
15 Canada
16 Armenia
17 Scotland
18 Ireland
19 Belgium
20 Italy

Name that Composer

Score /20

1 Edvard Grieg
2 Arthur Sullivan
3 Léo Delibes
4 Johann Strauss Jr
5 Giuseppe Verdi
6 Richard Wagner
7 Johannes Brahms
8 Max Bruch
9 Camille Saint-Saëns
10 Gabriel Fauré
11 Edward Elgar
12 Giacomo Puccini
13 Richard Strauss
14 Jean Sibelius
15 Sergei Rachmaninov
16 Claude Debussy
17 Maurice Ravel
18 Ralph Vaughan Williams
19 Frederick Delius
20 Sergei Prokofiev

Quick Fire (*Fiendish*)

Score /20

1 "New Art"
2 Rheims
3 Cambrai Cathedral
4 Waltham Abbey
5 *Cantiones Sacrae*
6 55 days
7 Apollo
8 Canterbury Cathedral
9 Jean-Baptiste Lully
10 Count Giacomo Durazzo
11 Anna Girò
12 Johann Christoph Bach
13 Duke of Saxe-Weimar
14 Anna Magdalena Wilcken
15 John Taylor
16 *Rinaldo*
17 Alessandro
18 South America
19 King Frederick the Great
20 *The Art of Keyboard Playing*

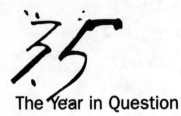

The Year in Question

Score **/20**

1 1902
2 1904
3 1905
4 1908
5 1910
6 1911
7 1912
8 1913
9 1914
10 1917
11 1918
12 1919
13 1920
14 1922
15 1924
16 1926
17 1927
18 1933
19 1934
20 1935

Mind the Gap

Score /20

1 *Trout*
2 *Cuckoo*
3 *Bird*
4 *Goose*
5 *Lark*
6 *Magpie*
7 *Swan*
8 *Swan*
9 *Swan*
10 *Vixen*
11 *Bee*
12 *Bumblebee*
13 *Butterfly*
14 *Wasps*
15 *Duckling*
16 *Sheep*
17 *Flea*
18 *Wolf*
19 *Animals*
20 *Elephant*

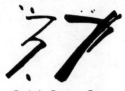

Odd One Out

Score   **/20**

1 Evgeny Kissin is a pianist and all the others are cellists.
2 The cornet is a brass instrument. All the others are percussion instruments.
3 Natalie Clein is a cellist and all the others are violinists.
4 Johann Sebastian is the father. The other four are his sons.
5 *Carmen* is an opera and all of the others are ballets.
6 *Carmen* was written by Bizet; all of the other operas were composed by Puccini.
7 All of these are genuine pieces written by Erik Satie, except for *Étude on Consideration of a Striped Ocelot,* which we made up.
8 *Parsifal* because, although it's an opera by Richard Wagner, it's not part of the *Ring* Cycle.
9 All the soundtracks to these films were written by John Williams, except for *Rain Man,* which was composed by Hans Zimmer.
10 Scarlatti, Bach and Handel were all born in 1685, but Zipoli was born in 1688.
11 All these operas were composed by Wolfgang Amadeus Mozart, except for *Turandot,* which was composed by Giacomo Puccini.
12 *Otello* was written by Giuseppe Verdi, but the other three are operas written by Gioachino Rossini.
13 Camille Saint-Saëns died at the age of 86; all the other three composers died while still in their thirties.
14 Gustav Mahler was the only one of these four composers not to die in an asylum.
15 Pyotr Ilyich Tchaikovsky – all the others were members of the group of Russian composers known as "The Mighty Handful".

16 The Italian Domenico Zipoli – all of the others were Czech.

17 Heitor Villa-Lobos, because, although all five of these composers are considered to be in the Spanish "nationalist school", Villa-Lobos was actually Brazilian.

18 *The Thieving Magpie* was written by Gioachino Rossini. All of the others were by W.S. Gilbert and Arthur Sullivan.

19 The American George Gershwin – all of the others were British.

20 The German Max Bruch – all of the others were French.

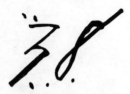

Quick Fire (*Fiendish*)

Score **/20**

1 Aloysia Weber
2 Pushkin
3 14
4 56
5 *Violin Tutor*
6 An opera company
7 37
8 144
9 Niccolò Paganini
10 He was a doctor
11 1833
12 Jean Françaix
13 Quarter-note
14 2,065
15 37
16 17
17 *A Life for the Tsar*
18 Nikolai Rimsky-Korsakov
19 Nadezhda von Meck
20 Five

Mix & Match

Score /20

1 Baroque
2 Modern
3 Romantic
4 Modern
5 Romantic
6 Modern
7 Romantic
8 Classical
9 Early
10 Early
11 Romantic
12 Baroque
13 Romantic
14 Modern
15 Romantic
16 Romantic
17 Early
18 Modern
19 Baroque
20 Romantic

Order! Order!

Score **/20**

1 Hildegard of Bingen (1098)
2 Claudio Monteverdi (1567)
3 Henry Purcell (1659)
4 Johann Sebastian Bach (1685)
5 Franz Joseph Haydn (1732)
6 Wolfgang Amadeus Mozart (1756)
7 Ludwig van Beethoven (1770)
8 Johann Strauss Sr (1804)
9 Felix Mendelssohn (1809)
10 César Franck (1822)
11 Max Bruch (1838)
12 Jules Massenet (1842)
13 Edvard Grieg (1843)
14 Edward Elgar (1857)
15 Igor Stravinsky (1882)
16 George Gershwin (1898)
17 Dmitri Shostakovich (1906)
18 Samuel Barber (1910)
19 Philip Glass (1937)
20 Patrick Hawes (1958)

Quick Fire (*Fiendish*)

Score /20

1 Director of the National Conservatory of Music
2 21 years: Johann Strauss Sr was born in 1804 and Johann Strauss Jr was born in 1825
3 A retirement home for musicians, which he had built in Milan
4 5 years: Johannes Brahms was born in 1833 and Max Bruch was born in 1838
5 Gabriel Fauré
6 A solicitor's
7 Edward Elgar's publisher, Augustus Jaeger
8 Arturo Toscanini
9 Vienna State Opera
10 *Aleko*
11 The highest mark in the institution's history: A++++
12 Dr Nikolai Dahl
13 Trombone
14 Thomas F. Ward
15 Eric Fenby
16 Arnold Schoenberg
17 Boston Symphony Orchestra
18 Kaplan
19 *Lady Macbeth of the Mtensk District*
20 Lowestoft

42

Mix & Match

Score /20

1 Antonio Salieri
2 Arnold Schoenberg
3 Bedřich Smetana
4 Franz Liszt
5 Frederick Delius
6 Gregorio Allegri
7 Hector Berlioz
8 Henryk Górecki
9 Isaac Albéniz
10 Jacopo Peri
11 Jacques Offenbach
12 Johannes Brahms
13 Louis Spohr
14 Maurice Ravel
15 Mikhail Glinka
16 Modest Mussorgsky
17 Nikolai Rimsky-Korsakov
18 Orlando Gibbons
19 Paul McCartney
20 Ralph Vaughan Williams

Whose Aria is it Anyway?

Score /20

1 Giacomo Puccini: *La Bohème*
2 Giuseppe Verdi: *La Traviata*
3 Giuseppe Verdi: *Il Trovatore*
4 Pyotr Ilyich Tchaikovsky: *Eugene Onegin*
5 Giuseppe Verdi: *Nabucco*
6 George Frideric Handel: *Semele*
7 Camille Saint-Saëns: *Samson and Delilah*
8 Giuseppe Verdi: *Rigoletto*
9 George Gershwin: *Porgy and Bess*
10 Giacomo Puccini: *Tosca*
11 Wolfgang Amadeus Mozart: *Don Giovanni*
12 Gaetano Donizetti: *L'elisir d'amore*
13 Christoph Willibald Gluck: *Orpheus and Euridice*
14 Wolfgang Amadeus Mozart: *The Magic Flute*
15 Giacomo Puccini: *La Rondine*
16 Giuseppe Verdi: *Rigoletto*
17 Wolfgang Amadeus Mozart: *The Marriage of Figaro*
18 Wolfgang Amadeus Mozart: *Don Giovanni*
19 Georges Bizet: *Carmen*
20 Giacomo Puccini: *Madam Butterfly*

Cinematic Sounds

Score /20

1 *The Silence of the Lambs*
2 *Platoon*
3 *A Clockwork Orange*
4 *Trainspotting*
5 *The Ladykillers*
6 *Bridget Jones's Diary*
7 *Out of Africa*
8 *The Shawshank Redemption*
9 *A Beautiful Mind*
10 *Natural Born Killers*
11 *A Room with a View*
12 *Bend it Like Beckham*
13 *Shine*
14 *Brassed Off*
15 *Babe*
16 *2001: A Space Odyssey*
17 *Billy Elliot*
18 *Pretty Woman*
19 *What's Opera, Doc?*
20 *Apocalypse Now*

Operatic Dons

Score   /20

1 *Lucrezia Borgia*
2 *Così fan tutte*
3 *The Gondoliers*
4 *The Barber of Seville*
5 *Les Indes Galantes*
6 *La Forza del Destino*
7 *The Marriage of Figaro*
8 *The Barber of Seville*
9 *Les Indes Galantes*
10 *La Finta Semplice*
11 *The Marriage of Figaro*
12 *Fidelio*
13 *Don Giovanni*
14 *Carmen*
15 *Koanga*
16 *Don Giovanni*
17 *Fidelio*
18 *La Finta Semplice*
19 *Don Quixote*
20 *Don Carlo; La Forza del Destino; Ernani*

Mix & Match

Score   **/16**

Christmas Carols

1 Felix Mendelssohn
2 Gustav Holst
3 Benjamin Britten
4 Ralph Vaughan Williams
5 Victor Hely-Hutchinson

Classical music eras:

1 Early
2 Baroque
3 Classical
4 Romantic
5 Modern

The Planets Suite:

1 War
2 Peace
3 Jollity
4 Magic
5 Old Age
6 Mysticism

The Year in Question

Score   **/20**

1 1936
2 1938
3 1942
4 1947
5 1948
6 1953
7 1958
8 1961
9 1971
10 1972
11 1975
12 1976
13 1985
14 1987
15 1989
16 1990
17 1992
18 1995
19 1996
20 1999

Order! Order!

Score /20

Musical notes:

1 Breve
2 Semibreve
3 Minim
4 Crotchet
5 Quaver
6 Semiquaver
7 Demisemiquaver
8 Hemidemisemiquaver

The *Ring* Cycle:

1 *Das Rheingold*
2 *Die Walküre*
3 *Siegfried*
4 *Götterdämmerung*

Stravinsky:

1 Russia
2 Switzerland
3 France
4 USA

Ballets:

1 *Giselle*
2 *Coppélia*
3 *The Sleeping Beauty*
4 *Pulcinella*

49

Name that Composer

Score **/20**

1 Francis Poulenc
2 George Gershwin
3 Aaron Copland
4 William Walton
5 Dmitri Shostakovich
6 Benjamin Britten
7 Leonard Bernstein
8 Arvo Pärt
9 John Tavener
10 Philip Glass
11 John Rutter
12 Karl Jenkins
13 Paul McCartney
14 Ludovico Einaudi
15 Joby Talbot
16 John Williams
17 John Barry
18 Howard Shore
19 James Horner
20 Hans Zimmer

Heavenly Music

Score /24

1 Sagittarius
2 Sagittarius
3 Taurus
4 Capricorn
5 Scorpio
6 Leo
7 Aquarius
8 Pisces
9 Gemini
10 Libra
11 Leo
12 Cancer
13 Gemini
14 Pisces
15 Aries
16 Virgo
17 Cancer
18 Aquarius
19 Virgo
20 Capricorn
21 Scorpio
22 Aries
23 Libra
24 Taurus

Grand Total Score /1000

Where To Find Out More About Classical Music

If this book has whetted your appetite to find out more, one of the best ways to discover what you like about classical music is to tune in to Classic FM. We broadcast 24 hours a day across the UK on 100–102 FM, and also on DAB Digital Radio and through digital satellite and cable television. You can also listen online at www.classicfm.com. We play a huge breadth of different classical music each week.

This book is one of a series published by Hodder Arnold. *The Classic FM Friendly Guide to Music* tells the story of classical music and our *Friendly Guides* to Mozart, Beethoven and Elgar allow you to understand the lives and music of each of these great composers in more depth. All of these books include a CD of excerpts of relevant classical music.

If you would like to delve far, far deeper into the subject, the universally acknowledged authority on the subject is *The New Grove Dictionary of Music and Musicians.* The original version was edited by Sir George Grove, with the eminent musicologist Stanley Sadie taking over the reins for this new edition (published in 1995). But be warned – this is a weighty tome, running to 20 hardback volumes with around 29,000 separate articles. You can also access the database online by subscribing to www.grovemusic.com.

In truth, this database is far more detailed than most music lovers would ever need; a more manageable reference book is *The Concise Oxford Dictionary of Music,* edited by Michael Kennedy (published by Oxford Reference), or *The Penguin Companion to Classical Music,* edited by Paul Griffiths (published by Penguin). Paul Griffiths has also written *A Concise History of Western Music* (published by Cambridge University Press) – a highly readable discussion of the way classical music evolved over time.

The *DK Eyewitness Companion to Classical Music*, edited by John Burrows (published by Dorling Kindersley), is a very colourful and reliable source of information on the chronology of classical music. For a slightly quirkier walk through the subject, we recommend *Stephen Fry's Incomplete & Utter History of Classical Music*, which is published by Macmillan and is based on the Classic FM radio series of the same name, written by Tim Lihoreau. We also hope that you enjoy the Classic FM book *Classic Ephemera* by Darren Henley and Tim Lihoreau (published by Boosey & Hawkes), which is packed full of classical music facts, stories and trivia.

For younger classical music lovers or discoverers, *The Story of Classical Music, Famous Composers* and *More Famous Composers* are all published by Naxos Audiobooks in association with Classic FM. These titles are aimed at 8- to 14-year-olds and contain musical excerpts and CD-ROM elements.

For up-to-the-minute news on the latest CD releases, *Classic FM Magazine* contains around 150 reviews each month. You might also enjoy reading *The Gramophone,* the magazine that many music enthusiasts regard as the last word in classical music criticism.

The very best way of finding out more about which pieces of classical music you like is by going out and hearing a live performance for yourself.

There is simply no substitute for seeing the whites of the eyes of a talented soloist as they perform a masterpiece on a stage only a few feet in front of you. Classic FM has a series of partnerships with orchestras across the country: the Royal Scottish National Orchestra, the Royal Liverpool Philharmonic Orchestra, the Philharmonia Orchestra and the London Symphony Orchestra. To see if they have a concert coming up somewhere near you, log on to www.classicfm.com and click on the "Concerts and Events" section.

Happy listening!

About the Author

Darren Henley began working as a newsreader at Classic FM in 1992, becoming Managing Editor in 2000 and Station Manager in 2004. Since 2006, he has been Managing Director of Classic FM and the new DAB Digital Radio station, theJazz. He has written 15 books about classical music and musicians. He began his career as a journalist at Invicta Radio in Kent and then at ITN.

The Sony Radio Academy Awards, the Arqiva Commercial Radio Awards, the British Radio Awards, the New York International Radio Festival and the United Nations have all honoured his radio programmes. The American Audiobook Publishers Association consecutively named two of his audiobooks for children, *The Story of Classical Music* and *Famous Composers*, as "best original work" in 2005 and 2006. Naxos Audiobooks publish both. *The Story of Classical Music* also won the *Radio Times* Readers' Choice Award at the British Spoken Word Awards in 2005 and was nominated for a Grammy Award.

He is the author of *The Classic FM Friendly Guide to Music* and the co-author of *The Classic FM Friendly Guide to Mozart, The Classic FM Friendly Guide to Beethoven* and *The Classic FM Friendly Guide to Elgar*, all published by Hodder Arnold.

CLASSIC *f*M

The *Friendly* Guide to

Mozart

Darren Henley and Tim Lihoreau

Wolfgang Amadeus Mozart is arguably the greatest composer who ever lived. In the 250 years since his birth, the popularity of his music has soared and he is now recognized around the world as being at the top of the classical music tree.

The Classic FM *Friendly Guide to Mozart* takes you by the hand and provides you with a *friendly* introduction to the man and his music. In true Classic FM style we have removed the jargon that sometimes surrounds classical music to give you a fun, accessible read.

Other *friendly* features are:
- a CD with excerpts from Mozart's Top 20 hits, as voted for by listeners to the Classic FM 'Hall of Fame'
- a Mozart Mood Chart
- a list of Mozart's movie music.

The Classic FM *Friendly Guide to Mozart* tells you everything you ever wanted to know about Mozart and his music.

£9.99 ISBN 978 0340 91395 6

CLASSIC *f*M

The *Friendly* Guide to

Beethoven

John Suchet and Darren Henley

Ludwig van Beethoven is without doubt one of the greatest composers who ever lived. He is also one of the most fascinating: his difficult childhood, the onset of deafness and his final lonely descent into a world of silence make his musical achievements all the more inspiring.

The Classic FM *Friendly Guide to Beethoven* takes you by the hand and provides you with a *friendly* introduction to this fiery, enigmatic man and his music.

Other *friendly* features are:

- a CD with excerpts from Beethoven's Top 20 hits, as voted for by listeners to the Classic FM 'Hall of Fame'
- a Beethoven Mood Chart
- a list of Beethoven's movie music.

The Classic FM *Friendly Guide to Beethoven* tells you everything you ever wanted to know about Beethoven and his music.

£9.99 ISBN 978 0340 92864 6

CLASSIC *f*M

The *Friendly* Guide to

Elgar

Tim Lihoreau and Darren Henley

Edward Elgar, born 150 years ago in 1857, was the greatest English composer of his age. He changed England from a land without music into a land of high hopes and musical glory – the original 'Cool Britannia'.

But besides being the highest-rating home-grown talent in the Classic FM Hall of Fame, was there more to this seemingly quintessential Englishman than meets the ear? The Classic FM *Friendly Guide to Elgar* answers a resounding YES.

This book takes you by the hand and provides you with a friendly introduction not just to the enigmatic music, but also to the passionate and private person. In true Classic FM style, we have junked the jargon that sometimes surrounds classical music to give you a fun, accessible read.

Other *friendly* features are:
- a CD with excerpts from Elgar's Top 20 hits, as voted for by listeners to the Classic FM 'Hall of Fame'
- an Elgar Mood Chart
- a list of Elgar's movie music.

The Classic FM *Friendly Guide to Elgar* tells you everything you ever wanted to know about Elgar and his music.

£9.99 ISBN 978 0340 93911 6

CLASSIC *f*M

The *Friendly* Guide to

Music

Darren Henley

The Classic FM *Friendly Guide to Music* is the book about classical music for people who wouldn't normally consider buying a book on the subject, but who are interested in developing a greater understanding of classical music. It gives a friendly, jargon-free overview of classical music from its earliest times right through to the present day, concentrating on the composers who are played regularly on Classic FM.

The Classic FM *Friendly Guide to Music* takes you on a journey through the five main eras of classical music: early, baroque, classical, romantic and contemporary. There are handy 'Instant Guides' to each of the main composers featured in the book and sections on

- music in films
- the Classic FM 'Hall of Fame'
- composers' quotes about each other.

Other *friendly* features are:

- a music timeline
- a music mood guide
- a CD with excerpts of the music so you can have a listen yourself.

The Classic FM *Friendly Guide to Music* will help you understand and enjoy the rich tapestry of sounds, emotions and stories which go together to make up classical music and its world.

£9.99 ISBN 978 0340 94019 8